SCHOLASTIC

BOOK OF WORLD RECORDS 2011

SCHOLASTIC INC.
NEW YORK • TORONTO • LONDON • AUCKLAND
SYDNEY • MEXICO CITY • NEW DELHI • HONG KONG

To Isabelle Nicole—May you always find wonder in the world.
—JCM

CREATED AND PRODUCED BY GEORGIAN BAY ASSOCIATES, LLC

Copyright © 2010 by Georgian Bay Associates
All rights reserved. Published by Scholastic Inc., *Publishers since 1920*.

SCHOLASTIC and associated logos are trademarks
and/or registered trademarks of Scholastic Inc.

GEORGIAN BAY STAFF
Bruce S. Glassman, Executive Editor
Jenifer Corr Morse, Photo Editor
Amy Stirnkorb, Designer

ISBN 978-0-545-23748-2

10 9 8 7 6 5 4 3 2 1   10 11 12 13 14
Printed in the U.S.A.   40
First printing, November 2010

In most cases, the graphs in this book represent the top five record holders in each category. However, in some graphs, we have chosen to list well-known or common people, places, animals, or things that will help you better understand how extraordinary the record holder is. These may not be the top five in the category. Additionally, some graphs have fewer than five entries because so few people or objects reflect the necessary criteria.

Due to the publication date, the majority of statistics is current as of May 2010.

CONTENTS

CONTENTS

POP CULTURE RECORDS

Television • Movies • Music • Magazines • Theater • Art

Highest-Paid TV Actor

CHARLIE SHEEN

Charlie Sheen gets $875,000 an episode for his role as Charlie Harper on the hit CBS sitcom *Two and a Half Men*, which he also helps produce. The Emmy-winning show is consistently one of the top-rated comedies each year. For this role, Sheen has been nominated for two Golden Globe Awards and four Emmy Awards. Before Sheen graced the TV screen, he appeared in many successful movies, including *Platoon* (1986), *Major League* (1989), *Hot Shots!* (1991), and *Scary Movie 3* (2003). Sheen got his star on the Hollywood Walk of Fame in 1994.

Highest-Paid TV Actors

Money earned per episode during the 2009–2010 season, in US dollars

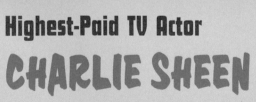

Charlie Sheen, *Two and a Half Men*	Kiefer Sutherland, *24*	Hugh Laurie, *House*	Christopher Meloni, *Law & Order SVU*	Alec Baldwin, *30 Rock*
875,000	550,000	400,000	400,000	300,000

Highest-Paid TV Actresses

THE DESPERATE HOUSEWIVES

Marcia Cross, Teri Hatcher, Felicity Huffman, and Eva Longoria Parker—the main cast of the hit show *Desperate Housewives*—each make $440,000 an episode. The ladies of Wisteria Lane are better known as Bree Hodge (Cross), Susan Mayer (Hatcher), Lynette Scavo (Huffman), and Gabrielle Solis (Longoria Parker) to television audiences. Executive producer Marc Cherry brought this nighttime soap to life in 2004, and since then the show has won seven Emmy Awards and three Golden Globes.

Highest-Paid TV Actresses

Money earned per episode during the 2009–2010 season, in US dollars

Marcia Cross, *Desperate Housewives*	Teri Hatcher, *Desperate Housewives*	Felicity Huffman, *Desperate Housewives*	Eva Longoria Parker, *Desperate Housewives*	Mariska Hargitay, *Law & Order: SVU*
440,000	440,000	440,000	440,000	400,000

Touch

Most Popular Television Show

AMERICAN IDOL RESULTS

More than 14 percent of the TV-viewing audience tuned in during the 2009 season to watch the weekly results for the eighth installment of *American Idol*. During this ultimate reality singing contest, viewers watched Kris Allen defeat Adam Lambert after fans cast nearly 100 million votes—the most votes in *Idol* history. Allen bested 35 other contestants and braved comments from judges Simon Cowell, Paula Abdul, Randy Jackson, and Kara DioGuardi. *American Idol* is one of just three television shows that have been rated number one for five consecutive seasons.

Most Popular Television Shows
Average audience percentage in 2009

American Idol Results	American Idol	Dancing with the Stars	Sunday Night Football	Dancing with the Stars Results
14.4	13.8	12.0	11.7	9.9

Highest-Paid Talk Show Host

OPRAH WINFREY

Oprah Winfrey pulled in $275 million in 2009, making her the world's highest-paid entertainer. In total, she is worth more than $1.5 billion. Winfrey's self-made millions have come mostly from her television show, which began in 1983. Since then, Winfrey has been educating her viewers and helping her audience with tough social issues. The megastar is also involved in movies, television production, magazines, books, radio, and the Internet. In 2011, she will debut the Oprah Winfrey Network. She began a three-year deal with XM Satellite Radio in 2009.

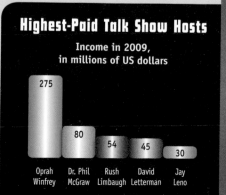

Highest-Paid Talk Show Hosts

Income in 2009, in millions of US dollars

Oprah Winfrey	Dr. Phil McGraw	Rush Limbaugh	David Letterman	Jay Leno
275	80	54	45	30

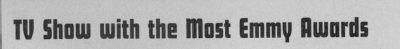

TV Show with the Most Emmy Awards

FRASIER

Frasier—a hugely popular show that ran between 1993 and 2004—picked up 37 Emmy Awards during its 11 seasons. The sitcom focused on the life and family of psychiatrist Dr. Frasier Crane, played by Kelsey Grammer. His co-stars included David Hyde Pierce, John Mahoney, Peri Gilpin, and Jane Leeves. Some of the 37 awards the series won include Outstanding Comedy Series, Lead Actor in a Comedy Series, Supporting Actor in a Comedy Series, Directing in a Comedy Series, Editing, and Art Direction.

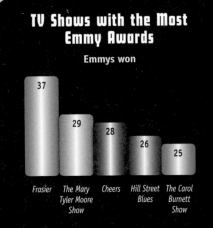

TV Shows with the Most Emmy Awards

Emmys won

Frasier	The Mary Tyler Moore Show	Cheers	Hill Street Blues	The Carol Burnett Show
37	29	28	26	25

THE DAILY SHOW WITH JON STEWART & THE AMAZING RACE

Two television shows—*The Daily Show with Jon Stewart* and *The Amazing Race*—are tied for the most consecutive Emmy wins with seven each. Comedy Central's *The Daily Show* is a fake news program and has been hosted by Jon Stewart since 1999. The show picked up Emmys for Outstanding Variety, Music, or Comedy Series, and Outstanding Writing for Outstanding Variety, Music or Comedy Program. *The Amazing Race* on CBS has won the Emmy for Outstanding Reality-Competition Program since the award was first given in 2003. The show is hosted by Phil Keoghan and produced by Jerry Bruckheimer.

TV Shows with the Most Consecutive Emmy Awards

Emmys won

The Daily Show with Jon Stewart, 2003–2009	The Amazing Race, 2003–2009	Frasier, 1994–1998	The Late Show with David Letterman, 1998–2002	The West Wing, 2000–2003
7	7	5	5	4

Jerry Bruckheimer (left) and Phil Keoghan

Male Performer with the Most Emmy Awards

CARL REINER

Veteran actor Carl Reiner has won eight Emmy Awards since his acting career began in the 1950s. In 1957, Reiner picked up his first Emmy for his work on the comedy *Caesar's Hour*. A year later, he got his second award for *Sid Caesar Invites You*. Then, beginning in 1962, Reiner won three consecutive Emmys for his role on *The Dick Van Dyke Show*. Later, Reiner was recognized for his television writing with two awards in 1965 and 1967 for his work on *The Dick Van Dyke Show* and *The Sid Caesar Show*. Almost 30 years later, Reiner picked up an Emmy for a guest spot he did on the comedy *Mad About You*. Reiner continues to entertain audiences today, most recently with his role as Saul Bloom in the Ocean's Eleven movies.

Male Performers with the Most Emmy Awards

Emmys won

Carl Reiner	Ed Asner	Alan Alda	Art Carney	Billy Crystal
9	7	6	6	6

Female Performer with the Most Emmy Awards

CLORIS LEACHMAN

Since her acting career began almost 40 years ago, comedian Cloris Leachman has won eight Emmy Awards. Leachman won her first three awards between 1973 and 1975 for her role on *The Mary Tyler Moore Show*. In 1975, she also won an Emmy for her work on the variety show *Cher*. In 1984, she picked up another Emmy for her performance on the *Screen Actors Guild 50th Anniversary Celebration*. In 1998, Leachman grabbed an Emmy for her guest spot on *Promised Land*. And in 2002 and 2006, she won two statues for guest spots on *Malcolm in the Middle*. In 2008, Leachman danced her way back into the television spotlight with a stint on *Dancing with the Stars*.

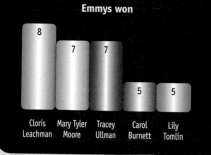

Female Performers with the Most Emmy Awards

Emmys won

Cloris Leachman	Mary Tyler Moore	Tracey Ullman	Carol Burnett	Lily Tomlin
8	7	7	5	5

Actor with the Most Oscar Nominations

JACK NICHOLSON

Jack Nicholson has been nominated for a record 12 Oscars during his distinguished career. He is one of only three men to have been nominated for an acting Academy Award at least once every decade for five decades. He was nominated for eight Best Actor awards for his roles in *Five Easy Pieces* (1970), *The Last Detail* (1973), *Chinatown* (1974), *One Flew Over the Cuckoo's Nest* (1975), *Prizzi's Honor* (1985), *Ironweed* (1987), *As Good As It Gets* (1997), and *About Schmidt* (2002). He was nominated for Best Supporting Actor for *Easy Rider* (1969), *Reds* (1981), *Terms of Endearment* (1983), and *A Few Good Men* (1992). Nicholson picked up statues for *One Flew Over the Cuckoo's Nest*, *Terms of Endearment*, and *As Good As It Gets*.

Actors with the Most Oscar Nominations

Oscar nominations

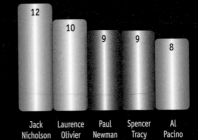

Jack Nicholson	Laurence Olivier	Paul Newman	Spencer Tracy	Al Pacino
12	10	9	9	8

Actress with the Most Oscar Nominations

MERYL STREEP

Meryl Streep is the most nominated actress in the history of the Academy Awards with 16 chances to win a statue. Her first nomination came in 1979 for *The Deer Hunter*, and was followed by *Kramer vs. Kramer* (1980), *The French Lieutenant's Woman* (1981), *Sophie's Choice* (1982), *Silkwood* (1983), *Out of Africa* (1985), *Ironweed* (1987), *A Cry in the Dark* (1988), *Postcards From the Edge* (1990), *The Bridges of Madison County* (1995), *One True Thing* (1998), *Music of the Heart* (1999), *Adaptation* (2002), *The Devil Wears Prada* (2006), *Doubt* (2008), and *Julie and Julia* (2009). Streep won her first Academy Award for *Kramer vs. Kramer*, and followed with a second win for *Sophie's Choice*.

Actresses with the Most Oscar Nominations

Oscar nominations

Meryl Streep	Katharine Hepburn	Bette Davis	Geraldine Page	Greer Garson
16	12	10	8	7

Presenters and the cast of *The Lord of the Rings* (Peter Jackson in front)

Movies with the Most Oscars

BEN-HUR, TITANIC, & THE LORD OF THE RINGS: THE RETURN OF THE KING

The only three films in Hollywood history to win 11 Academy Awards are *Ben-Hur*, *Titanic*, and *The Lord of the Rings: The Return of the King*. Some of the Oscar wins for *Ben-Hur*—a biblical epic based on an 1880 novel by General Lew Wallace—include Best Actor (Charlton Heston) and Director (William Wyler). Some of *Titanic*'s Oscars include Best Cinematography, Visual Effects, and Costume Design. *The Lord of the Rings: The Return of the King* is the final film in the epic trilogy based on the works of J. R. R. Tolkien. With 11 awards, it is the most successful movie in Academy Awards history because it won every category in which it was nominated. Some of these wins include Best Picture, Director (Peter Jackson), and Costume Design.

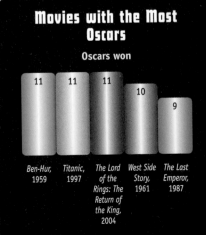

Movies with the Most Oscars

Oscars won

Ben-Hur, 1959	Titanic, 1997	The Lord of the Rings: The Return of the King, 2004	West Side Story, 1961	The Last Emperor, 1987
11	11	11	10	9

Actor with the Most MTV Movie Awards

JIM CARREY

Jim Carrey has won 11 MTV Movie Awards since the television station began awarding them in 1992. He has won the award for Best Comedic Performance six times for his roles in *Dumb & Dumber* (1995), *Ace Ventura II: When Nature Calls* (1996), *The Cable Guy* (1997), *Liar Liar* (1998), *How the Grinch Stole Christmas* (2001), and *Yes Man* (2009). Carrey won the award for Best Male Performance twice for *Ace Ventura II: When Nature Calls* and *The Truman Show* (1999). He also won awards for Best Kiss for *Dumb & Dumber*, Best Villain for *The Cable Guy*, and the MTV Generation Award in 2006.

Actors with the Most MTV Movie Awards

Awards won

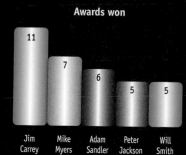

Jim Carrey	Mike Myers	Adam Sandler	Peter Jackson	Will Smith
11	7	6	5	5

Uma Thurman

Actresses with the Most MTV Movie Awards

ALICIA SILVERSTONE & UMA THURMAN

Alicia Silverstone and Uma Thurman are tied for the most MTV Movie Awards with four statues apiece. Silverstone won her first two awards—Best Villain and Breakthrough Performance—in 1994 for her movie *The Crush*. She picked up two more in 1996—Best Female Performance and Most Desirable Female—for her role in *Clueless*. Thurman won a Best Dance Sequence award in 1995 for *Pulp Fiction*. She won Best Female Performance and Best Fight (with Chiaki Kuriyama) in 2004 for *Kill Bill I*. A year later she picked up a second Best Fight award for *Kill Bill II*.

Actresses with the Most MTV Movie Awards

Awards won

Alicia Silverstone	Uma Thurman	Drew Barrymore	Kirsten Dunst	Cameron Díaz
4	4	3	3	3

Actor with the Highest Average Box-Office Gross
STAN LEE

Appearing in 14 movies since he debuted as an actor in 1995, Stan Lee rules the box office with an average gross of $184.1 million per movie. Some of his biggest films include the Spider-Man trilogy, which earned a combined $2.5 billion worldwide. Lee is the co-creator of the Spider-Man comic book series for Marvel Comics, and was given small parts in all of the films. He also helped create the Iron Man, Fantastic Four, X-Men, and Hulk comic books, and was able to appear in those films as well. Lee has been honored for his work numerous times, including by induction into the Jack Kirby Hall of Fame, with a National Medal of Arts, and with a Comic-Con Icon Award at the Scream Awards.

Actors with the Highest Average Box-Office Gross

Average box-office gross, in millions of US dollars

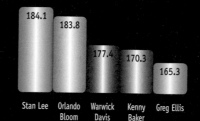

Stan Lee	Orlando Bloom	Warwick Davis	Kenny Baker	Greg Ellis
184.1	183.8	177.4	170.3	165.3

Actor with the Highest Career Box-Office Gross

FRANK WELKER

Frank Welker's movies have a combined total gross of $5.72 billion. Although movie fans might not recognize Welker's name or face, they would probably recognize one of his voices. Welker is a voice actor, and has worked on 91 movies in the last 25 years. Some of his most famous voices include Megatron, Curious George, and Scooby-Doo. Welker's most profitable movies include *How the Grinch Stole Christmas*, *Godzilla*, and *101 Dalmatians*.

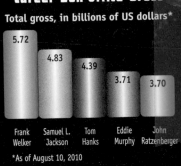

Actors with the Highest Career Box-Office Gross

Total gross, in billions of US dollars*

Frank Welker	Samuel L. Jackson	Tom Hanks	Eddie Murphy	John Ratzenberger
5.72	4.83	4.39	3.71	3.70

*As of August 10, 2010

Top-Grossing Animated Movie
SHREK 2

Since it opened in May 2004, *Shrek 2* has brought in more than $919 million worldwide. The second movie in the Shrek series starred Mike Myers as Shrek, Cameron Diaz as Princess Fiona, Eddie Murphy as Donkey, and Antonio Banderas as Puss-in-Boots. It was the eighth highest-grossing opening weekend ever, earning $128.9 million in just three days. It was also the ninth-biggest opening day in history with $94.1 million. *Shrek 2* was nominated for two Oscars, a Golden Globe, two Grammy Awards, and four Kids' Choice Awards.

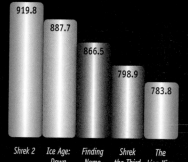

Top-Grossing Animated Movies

Total worldwide gross, in millions of US dollars

Shrek 2	Ice Age: Dawn of the Dinosaurs	Finding Nemo	Shrek the Third	The Lion King
919.8	887.7	866.5	798.9	783.8

Movie with the Most Successful Opening Weekend

THE DARK KNIGHT

On July 18, 2008, *The Dark Knight* opened in theaters and pulled in $158.4 million in just one weekend. The blockbuster movie, which is the sequel to *Batman Begins*, starred Christian Bale as Batman, Maggie Gyllenhaal as Rachel Dawes, Aaron Eckhart as Harvey Dent, and Heath Ledger as The Joker. *The Dark Knight* was released in 4,366 theaters and broke the record for a movie's largest release. The movie brought in $67.1 million on its opening day, with $18.5 million coming from midnight screenings. Heath Ledger won a Golden Globe and an Oscar posthumously for his role in the film.

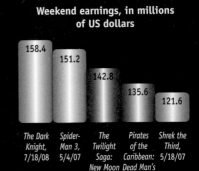

Movies with the Most Successful Opening Weekends

Weekend earnings, in millions of US dollars

Movie	Earnings
The Dark Knight, 7/18/08	158.4
Spider-Man 3, 5/4/07	151.2
The Twilight Saga: New Moon 11/20/09	142.8
Pirates of the Caribbean: Dead Man's Chest, 7/7/06	135.6
Shrek the Third, 5/18/07	121.6

Top-Grossing Movie
AVATAR

Avatar, James Cameron's science-fiction epic, was released in December 2009 and grossed more than $2.71 billion worldwide in less than two months. Starring Sigourney Weaver, Sam Worthington, and Zoe Saldana, *Avatar* cost more than $230 million to make. Cameron began working on the film in 1994, and it was eventually filmed in 3-D, with special cameras made just for the movie. Due to *Avatar*'s overwhelming success, Cameron is already planning a sequel.

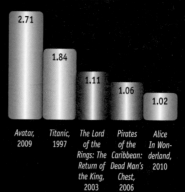

Top-Grossing Movies
Total worldwide gross, in billions of US dollars*

Avatar, 2009	Titanic, 1997	The Lord of the Rings: The Return of the King, 2003	Pirates of the Caribbean: Dead Man's Chest, 2006	Alice In Wonderland, 2010
2.71	1.84	1.11	1.06	1.02

*As of August 10, 2010

Top Moviegoing Country

UNITED STATES

American moviegoers spend more than $10.4 billion each year on trips to the big screen. The average American sees about four movies annually. That equals about 1.5 billion admissions annually, with an average ticket price of $7.22. Some 600 movies are released throughout the country each year. When a new movie is released, it runs in theaters for about eight weeks and is shown on about 2,000 screens.

Top Moviegoing Countries

2009 box-office revenue, in billions of US dollars

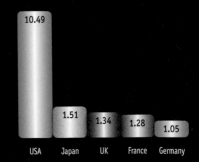

USA	Japan	UK	France	Germany
10.49	1.51	1.34	1.28	1.05

Country with the Most Movie Screens
UNITED STATES

There are about 39,233 movie screens located in nearly 6,000 movie theaters throughout the United States. About 628 screens are at drive-ins, and the other 38,605 screens are indoor theaters. Since the first permanent electric theater opened in 1902, Americans have flocked to the big screen. Megaplexes, or large movie theaters that show several movies at the same time, are the most popular type of theater in the country. Approximately 1.5 billion movie tickets are sold in the United States each year.

Countries with the Most Movie Screens
Number of screens

USA	India	France	Germany	China
39,233	10,410	5,400	5,000	4,700

25

Top-Earning Actor
DANIEL RADCLIFFE

Daniel Radcliffe—best known for his title role in the Harry Potter movies—earned $41 million during 2009. *Harry Potter and the Half-Blood Prince*, the series' sixth installment, was released in July 2009 and made more than $933 million worldwide. Radcliffe has appeared on the *Sunday Times* Rich List in the UK several times since 2006. He also earned rave reviews for his role as Alan Strang in the play *Equus* in 2007 and 2008. He won two Broadway.com Audience Awards for that role.

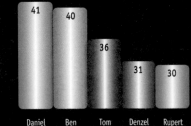

Top-Earning Actors

2009 earnings, in millions of US dollars

Daniel Radcliffe	Ben Stiller	Tom Hanks	Denzel Washington	Rupert Grint
41	40	36	31	30

Top-Earning Actress
EMMA WATSON

British actress Emma Watson earned $30 million during 2009. Famous for her role as Hermione Granger in the Harry Potter films, Watson has co-starred in all six movies in the series. For her performance, she has won a Young Artist Award and a National Movie Award. She has also been nominated for a Saturn Award, an Empire Award, a Scream Award, and two MTV Movie Awards. In addition to acting, Watson began modeling for Burberry in 2009.

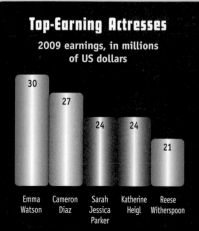

Top-Earning Actresses

2009 earnings, in millions of US dollars

Emma Watson	Cameron Diaz	Sarah Jessica Parker	Katherine Heigl	Reese Witherspoon
30	27	24	24	21

27

Highest Animated Film Budget

DISNEY'S A CHRISTMAS CAROL

In 2009, Disney put up a huge chunk of change to create *A Christmas Carol*, budgeting $200 million for the animated holiday classic. The movie—which was released in November 2009—starred Jim Carrey as the main character, Ebenezer Scrooge. The film was produced using performance capture, which records subtle movements and facial expressions. *A Christmas Carol* was released in 3-D and IMAX 3-D. The movie earned more than $323 million worldwide.

Highest Animated Film Budgets

Budget, in millions of US dollars

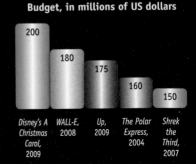

Disney's A Christmas Carol, 2009	WALL-E, 2008	Up, 2009	The Polar Express, 2004	Shrek the Third, 2007
200	180	175	160	150

Highest Movie Budget

PIRATES OF THE CARIBBEAN: AT WORLD'S END

With a budget of $300 million, the creators of *Pirates of the Caribbean: At World's End* spent the most money in movie history. And all of that money seems to have paid off. The third installment of the Pirates series opened in May 2007 and has since earned more than $960 million worldwide. It is the fifth-highest-grossing movie worldwide, and was the fourth-highest domestic gross in 2007. The Jerry Bruckheimer blockbuster starred Johnny Depp as Captain Jack Sparrow, Orlando Bloom as Will Turner, and Keira Knightley as Elizabeth Swann.

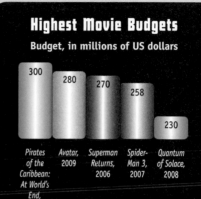

Highest Movie Budgets

Budget, in millions of US dollars

Pirates of the Caribbean: At World's End, 2007	Avatar, 2009	Superman Returns, 2006	Spider-Man 3, 2007	Quantum of Solace, 2008
300	280	270	258	230

Movie that Earned the Most in a Single Day

THE TWILIGHT SAGA: NEW MOON

Summit Entertainment's second installment of the Twilight Saga—*New Moon*—earned a record $72.7 million on November 20, 2009. The movie also earned the most money during a midnight screening with $26.3 million. The vampire romance movie was released in 4,024 theaters, with an average gross of $18,068 per theater. Many theaters were already sold out of tickets for the premiere two months before the big day. The movie went on to earn more than $295 million in the United States and a total of $705.5 million worldwide. *New Moon* starred Robert Pattinson, Kristen Stewart, and Taylor Lautner.

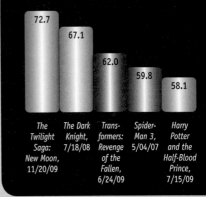

Movies that Earned the Most in a Single Day

Box-office earnings, in millions of US dollars

72.7	67.1	62.0	59.8	58.1
The Twilight Saga: New Moon, 11/20/09	The Dark Knight, 7/18/08	Trans-formers: Revenge of the Fallen, 6/24/09	Spider-Man 3, 5/04/07	Harry Potter and the Half-Blood Prince, 7/15/09

When you can live forever, what do you live for?

Top-Selling DVD
TWILIGHT

Twilight—the first installment of the teen vampire series that took the country by storm in 2008—became the top-selling DVD of 2009. The DVD sold about 10.2 million copies and made more than $186.2 million. The love story revolves around vampire Edward Cullen, played by Robert Pattinson, and mortal Bella Swan, played by Kristen Stewart. Summit Entertainment released the film, which is based on the bestselling book by Stephenie Meyer. The movie won five MTV Awards, ten Teen Choice Awards, and four Scream Awards.

Top-Selling DVDs
Units sold, in millions

Twilight	Transformers: Revenge of the Fallen	Up	Madagascar: Escape 2 Africa	Harry Potter and the Half-Blood Prince
10.23	9.26	8.44	7.78	6.66

Highest-Paid Director/Producer

MICHAEL BAY

Producer Michael Bay made a whopping $125 million in 2009. Bay's major film of the year was *Transformers: Revenge of the Fallen*, which earned more than $835 million worldwide. Some of Bay's other 2009 projects included *The Unborn* and *Friday the 13th*. Bay is a member and part-owner of three production houses—Digital Domain, Platinum Dunes, and The Institute. He has won five MTV Movie Awards, for the films *Transformers, Pearl Harbor, Bad Boys II*, and *The Rock*.

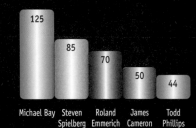

Highest-Paid Directors/Producers

Income in 2009, in millions of US dollars

Michael Bay	Steven Spielberg	Roland Emmerich	James Cameron	Todd Phillips
125	85	70	50	44

Most Downloaded Song

"BOOM BOOM POW"

"Boom Boom Pow"—the first single released off the Black Eyed Peas' album *The E.N.D.*—was the most downloaded song of 2009, with 4.76 million purchases. The song became the group's first number-one song in the United States when it peaked on the Billboard Hot 100 chart. The song sold 4.29 million copies in the United States in just 23 weeks, becoming the fastest-selling song in digital history. The song was also nominated for two Grammy Awards: Best Dance Recording and Best Short Form Music Video.

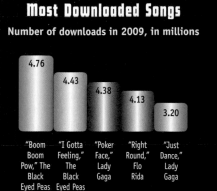

Most Downloaded Songs
Number of downloads in 2009, in millions

"Boom Boom Pow," The Black Eyed Peas	"I Gotta Feeling," The Black Eyed Peas	"Poker Face," Lady Gaga	"Right Round," Flo Rida	"Just Dance," Lady Gaga
4.76	4.43	4.38	4.13	3.20

Most Downloaded Recording Artist
LADY GAGA

Lady Gaga's songs were in high demand in 2009, grabbing the top spot with almost 15.3 million digital tracks sold. Some of the singer's most popular songs are "Just Dance," "Poker Face," "Paparazzi," and "Bad Romance." Her debut album, entitled *The Fame*, was released in August 2008 and quickly hit number one in four countries. She followed that up with *The Fame Monster* in 2009, and kicked off the Monster Ball Tour. By the end of 2009, Lady Gaga had sold more than 8 million albums and 35 million digital singles across the globe.

Most Downloaded Recording Artists

Total number of songs downloaded in 2009, in millions

Lady Gaga	The Black Eyed Peas	Michael Jackson	Taylor Swift	Beyoncé
15.29	12.98	12.35	12.30	9.26

Bestselling Digital Album

THE FAME

Lady Gaga's album *The Fame* was the bestselling digital album of 2009, with 461,000 downloads. Released in August 2008, *The Fame* reached number one in Ireland, Canada, and the United Kingdom, and number two on the Billboard 200 chart. Lady Gaga launched her Fame Ball Tour in March 2009 to promote the album. She was nominated for nine MTV Music Awards in 2009. She won three, including Best New Artist, Best Direction, and Best Editing.

Bestselling Digital Albums
Total number of downloads in 2009

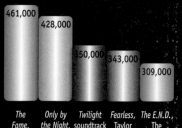

The Fame, Lady Gaga	Only by the Night, Kings of Leon	Twilight soundtrack	Fearless, Taylor Swift	The E.N.D., The Black Eyed Peas
461,000	428,000	350,000	343,000	309,000

Top-Selling Recording Artist
MICHAEL JACKSON

With almost $8.3 million in album sales during 2009, the legendary Michael Jackson was the bestselling artist of the year. The King of Pop, who passed away in June of 2009, had intended to launch a new tour and album later in the year. The album—*This Is It*—was released in October and contained 12 new tracks and 4 from previous albums. A documentary film about the singer, entitled *Michael Jackson's This Is It*, was released soon after. Both were hugely successful, and the film went on to become the highest-grossing documentary in history, with more than $259 million in box-office receipts.

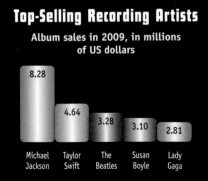

Top-Selling Recording Artists

Album sales in 2009, in millions of US dollars

Michael Jackson	Taylor Swift	The Beatles	Susan Boyle	Lady Gaga
8.28	4.64	3.28	3.10	2.81

United States' Bestselling Recording Group

THE BEATLES

The Beatles have sold 170 million copies of their albums in the United States since their first official recording session in September 1962. In the two years that followed, they had 26 Top 40 singles. John Lennon, Paul McCartney, George Harrison, and Ringo Starr made up the "Fab Four," as the Beatles were known. Together they recorded many albums that are now considered rock masterpieces, such as *Rubber Soul, Sgt. Pepper's Lonely Hearts Club Band*, and *The Beatles*. The group broke up in 1969. In 2001, however, their newly released greatest hits album—*The Beatles 1*—reached the top of the charts. One of their best-known songs—"Yesterday"—is the most recorded song in history, with about 2,500 different artists recording their own versions.

United States' Bestselling Recording Groups

Albums sold, in millions

The Beatles	Led Zeppelin	The Eagles	Pink Floyd	AC/DC
170.0	111.5	100.0	74.5	71.0

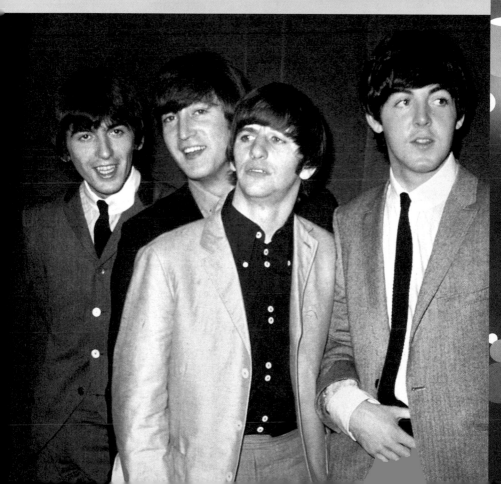

United States' Bestselling Male Recording Artist

GARTH BROOKS

Garth Brooks has sold 128 million albums since his professional career began in 1989. Brooks's career skyrocketed in 1991, when his third album—*Ropin' the Wind*—became the first country music album to debut on the top of the pop charts. From 1996 to 1999, Garth's tour stopped at 350 venues in 100 cities. More than 5.3 million tickets were sold, and it is considered one of the most successful tours in history. When the tour finished, Garth released his *Double Live* CD, and it became the bestselling live album ever. In all, Brooks has released 31 albums to date, and has won 15 Academy of Country Music Awards.

United States' Bestselling Male Recording Artists

Albums sold, in millions

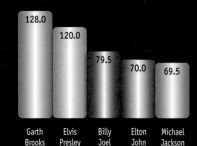

Garth Brooks	Elvis Presley	Billy Joel	Elton John	Michael Jackson
128.0	120.0	79.5	70.0	69.5

United States' Bestselling Female Recording Artist
BARBRA STREISAND

Barbra Streisand has sold more than 71 million copies of her work during her 39 years as a singer. She has recorded more than 50 albums and has more gold albums—or albums that have sold at least 500,000 copies—than any other entertainer in history. Streisand has 47 gold albums, 28 platinum albums, and 13 multiplatinum albums. Some of her recordings include "I Finally Found Someone" (1996), "Tell Him" (1997), and "If You Ever Leave Me" (1999). Some of her best-known film work includes roles in *Funny Girl*, *The Way We Were*, *Yentl*, and *Meet the Fockers*. Streisand has won 10 Grammys, 2 Academy Awards, 6 Emmy Awards, and 11 Golden Globes.

United States' Bestselling Female Recording Artists

Albums sold, in millions

Artist	Albums sold (millions)
Barbra Streisand	71.5
Madonna	64.0
Mariah Carey	62.5
Whitney Houston	55.0
Celine Dion	50.0

Top-Earning Male Singer
BRUCE SPRINGSTEEN

Bruce Springsteen—also known as "The Boss"—was the top-earning male musician in 2009, with $70 million. Springsteen kicked off the year by releasing his 16th studio album, *Working on a Dream*. It has sold 3 million copies worldwide and became the 9th number-one album of the year. In January 2009, he opened "We Are One: The Obama Inaugural Celebration at the Lincoln Memorial," and won a Golden Globe for Best Original Song for the title song from *The Wrestler*. He also performed at the Super Bowl halftime show and launched his worldwide Working on a Dream Tour.

Top-Earning Male Singers
Income in 2009, in millions of US dollars

Bruce Springsteen	Kenny Chesney	Toby Keith	Jay-Z	Kanye West
70	65	52	35	25

Top-Earning Female Singer
MADONNA

Legendary pop icon Madonna hauled in an impressive $110 million during 2009. In mid-2008, Madonna released her 11th studio album, *Hard Candy*, which debuted at number one in 37 different countries. She also kicked off her Sticky & Sweet Tour, and it became the highest-grossing solo artist tour in history. In 2009, Madonna released her 3rd greatest hits album, called *Celebration*. It contained some new songs, as well as 34 hits from the last few decades.

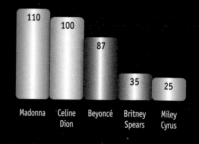

Top-Earning Female Singers

Income in 2009, in millions of US dollars

Madonna	Celine Dion	Beyoncé	Britney Spears	Miley Cyrus
110	100	87	35	25

Most Played Song
"YOU BELONG WITH ME"

"You Belong with Me," the third single released from Taylor Swift's album *Fearless*, was the most played radio song in 2009, with 465,100 airings. The song was released on the radio in April 2009 and quickly became Swift's eighth top-ten country hit. It also peaked at number two on the Billboard Hot 100 chart. The video for "You Belong with Me" won Swift Best Female Video at the Video Music Awards that year. It also received three Grammy nominations, for Song of the Year, Record of the Year, and Best Female Pop Vocal Performance.

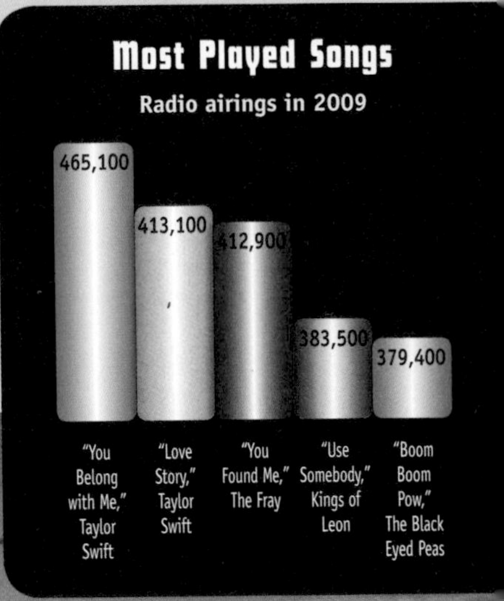
Most Played Songs
Radio airings in 2009
465,100
413,100
412,900
383,500
379,400
"You Belong with Me," Taylor Swift
"Love Story," Taylor Swift
"You Found Me," The Fray
"Use Somebody," Kings of Leon
"Boom Boom Pow," The Black Eyed Peas

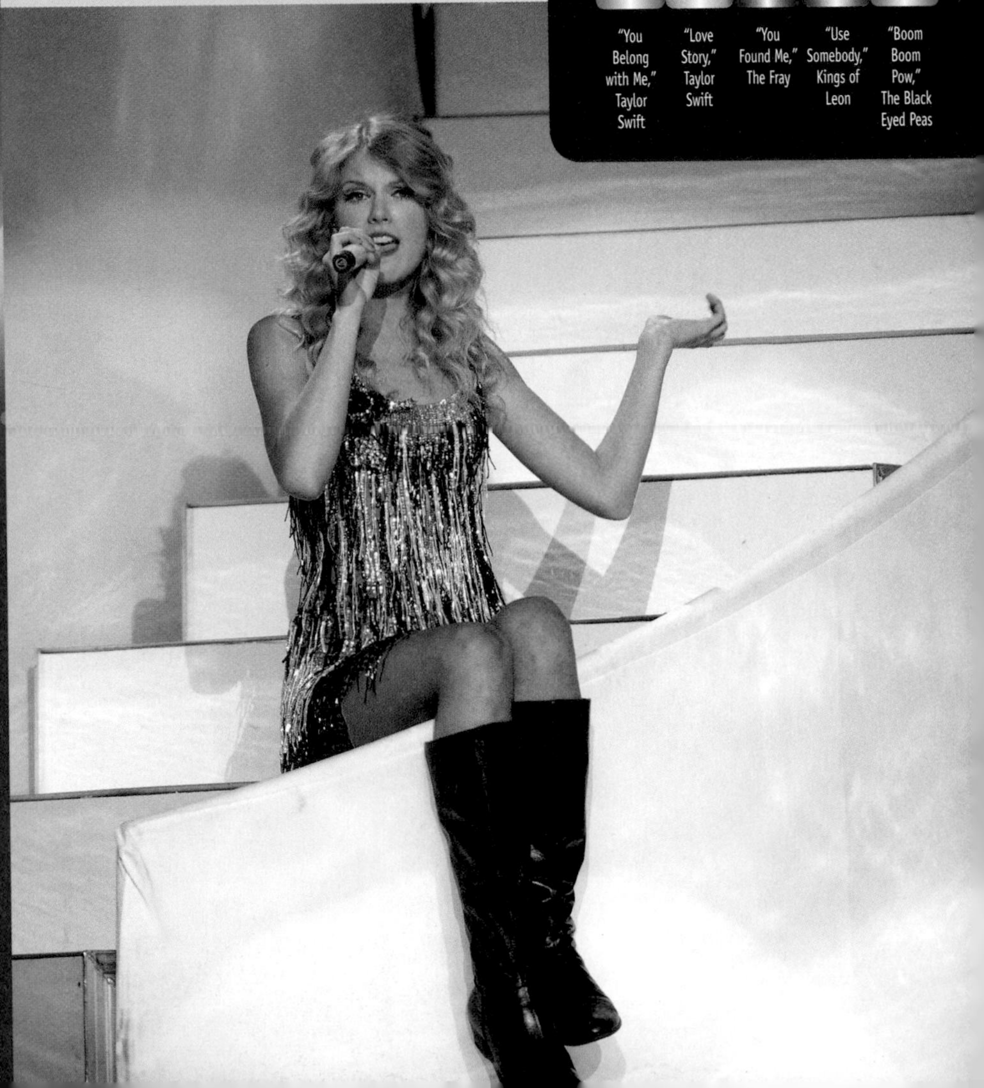

Bestselling Album

FEARLESS

Fearless—the second album released by country sensation Taylor Swift—flew off the shelves in 2009, finishing the year with more than 3.2 million copies sold. The album, which was released in November 2008, was the third-highest-selling album of that year, with 1.5 million copies sold. In fact, *Fearless* appeared at number one on the Billboard 200 for 11 nonconsecutive weeks. In 2010, Swift became the most downloaded artist in music history after she sold more than 24.3 million digital tracks. She also picked up a Grammy for Album of the Year.

Bestselling Albums

Albums sold in 2009, in millions

Fearless, Taylor Swift	3.21
I Dreamed a Dream, Susan Boyle	3.10
Number Ones, Michael Jackson	2.36
The Fame, Lady Gaga	2.24
My Christmas, Andrea Bocelli	2.21

Top-Earning Tour

U2

With $123 million in ticket sales, U2 scored the top-earning concert tour of 2009. The group kicked off their 360° Tour on June 30, 2009. As the name suggests, the concerts took place on stages that the fans could completely surround. The tour supported U2's *No Line on the Horizon* album. An October concert in California was recorded and streamed live on YouTube, which had never been done before. The total earnings of all of U2's concerts rank them as the second-highest-earning band of the decade.

Top-Earning Tours

Earnings in 2009, in millions of US dollars

U2	Bruce Springsteen and the E Street Band	Elton John/ Billy Joel	Britney Spears	AC/DC
123.0	94.5	88.0	82.5	77.9

Act with the Most Country Music Awards

GEORGE STRAIT

George Strait has won a whopping 22 Country Music Awards and has been nicknamed the "King of Country" for all of his accomplishments in the business. He won his first CMA award in 1985, and his most recent in 2008. In addition to his many awards, Strait holds the record for the most number one hits on the Billboard Hot Country Songs with 44. He also has 38 hit albums, including 12 multiplatinum and 22 platinum records. He was inducted into the Country Music Hall of Fame in 2006.

Acts with the Most Country Music Awards

Total awards won

George Strait	Brooks & Dunn	Vince Gill	Alan Jackson	Brad Paisley
22	19	18	16	13

Musician with the Most MTV Video Music Awards

MADONNA

Madonna has won 20 MTV Video Music Awards since the ceremony was first held in 1984. She has won four Cinematography awards, three Female Video awards, three Directing awards, two Editing awards, and two Art Direction awards. She also picked up single awards for Video of the Year, Choreography, Special Effects, and Long Form Video, as well as a Viewer's Choice and a Video Vanguard Award. Madonna's award-winning videos include "Papa Don't Preach," "Like a Prayer," "Express Yourself," "Vogue," "Rain," "Take a Bow," "Ray of Light," and "Beautiful Stranger."

Musicians with the Most MTV Video Music Awards

Total awards won

Madonna	Peter Gabriel	R.E.M.	Green Day	Aerosmith
20	13	12	11	10

Bestselling Kids' Magazines
SEVENTEEN & HIGHLIGHTS

Two kids' magazines—*Seventeen* and *Highlights*—each sell about 2 million copies per issue. First published in 1944, *Seventeen* is now part of the Hearst Magazine group and is targeted to 14- to 20-year-old women. It offers teens articles and advice on fashion, beauty, and health, as well as horoscopes and quizzes. *Highlights*, which is geared to a younger audience, was launched in 1946 and offers 5- to 12-year-olds stories, jokes, poems, hidden picture puzzles, and science features.

Bestselling Kids' Magazines

Number of copies
sold per issue, in millions

2.0	2.0	1.4	1.3	1.2
Seventeen	Highlights	Cosmo Girl	National Geographic for Kids	Boys' Life

Play with the Most Tony Awards
THE PRODUCERS

In March 2001, *The Producers* took home 12 of its record-breaking 15 Tony Award nominations. The Broadway smash won awards for Musical, Original Score, Book, Direction of a Musical, Choreography, Orchestration, Scenic Design, Costume Design, Lighting Design, Actor in a Musical, Featured Actor in a Musical, and Actress in a Musical. *The Producers*, which originally starred Nathan Lane and Matthew Broderick, is a stage adaptation of Mel Brooks's 1968 movie. Brooks wrote the lyrics and music for 16 new songs for the stage version.

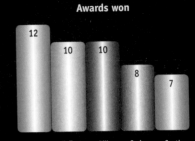

Plays with the Most Tony Awards
Awards won

The Producers, 2001	Hello, Dolly! 1964	Billy Elliot, 2009	Spring Awakening, 2007	South Pacific, 2008
12	10	10	8	7

Longest-Running Broadway Show

THE PHANTOM OF THE OPERA

The Phantom of the Opera has been performed more than 9,371 times since it opened in January 1988. The show tells the story of a disfigured musical genius who terrorizes the performers of the Paris Opera House. More than 100 million people have seen a performance in 149 cities and more than 25 countries. The show won seven Tony Awards its opening year, including Best Musical. The musical drama is performed at the Majestic Theater.

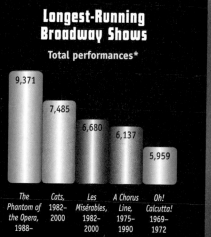

Longest-Running Broadway Shows
Total performances*

The Phantom of the Opera, 1988–	Cats, 1982–2000	Les Misérables, 1982–2000	A Chorus Line, 1975–1990	Oh! Calcutta! 1969–1972
9,371	7,485	6,680	6,137	5,959

*As of August 10, 2010

On the Interstate, 1956–1990

United States' Most-Visited Museum

NATIONAL MUSEUM OF AMERICAN HISTORY

Each year more than 7.4 million visitors pass through the doors of the National Museum of American History in Washington, DC, to learn about America's past. The vast museum has about 3 million artifacts in its collections, which range from Art to Government to Popular Entertainment. The museum, which opened in 1964, measures about 750,000 square feet (69,677 sq m). Some of the more unusual objects housed in the museum include Muhammad Ali's boxing gloves and robe, Evel Knievel's Harley-Davidson, and a Dumbo the Flying Elephant car from the ride in Disneyland.

United States' Most-Visited Museums

Annual attendance, in millions

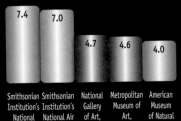

7.4	7.0	4.7	4.6	4.0
Smithsonian Institution's National Museum of American History, Washington	Smithsonian Institution's National Air and Space Museum, Washington	National Gallery of Art, Washington	Metropolitan Museum of Art, New York	American Museum of Natural History, New York

SPORTS RECORDS

Basketball • Football • Bicycling • Golf • Baseball
Track & Field • Tennis • Olympics • Figure Skating
Soccer • Car Racing • Motorcycling • Horse Racing
Hockey • X Games • Snowboarding

NBA Team with the Most Championship Titles

BOSTON CELTICS

The Boston Celtics are the most successful team in the NBA with 17 championship wins. The first win came in 1957, and the team went on to win the next seven consecutive titles—the longest streak of consecutive championship wins in the history of US sports. The most recent championship title came in 2008. The Celtics entered the Basketball Association of America in 1946, which later merged into the NBA in 1949. The Celtics made the NBA play-offs for four consecutive seasons from 2001 to 2005, but they were eliminated in early rounds each time.

NBA Teams with the Most Championship Titles

Number of championship titles

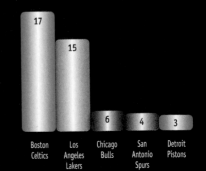

Boston Celtics	Los Angeles Lakers	Chicago Bulls	San Antonio Spurs	Detroit Pistons
17	15	6	4	3

NBA Player with the Highest Career Scoring Average

WILT CHAMBERLAIN & MICHAEL JORDAN

Both Michael Jordan and Wilt Chamberlain averaged an amazing 30.1 points per game during their legendary careers. Jordan played for the Chicago Bulls and the Washington Wizards. He led the league in scoring for seven years. During the 1986 season, he became the second person ever to score 3,000 points in a single season. Chamberlain played for the Philadelphia Warriors, the Philadelphia 76ers, and the Los Angeles Lakers. In addition to the highest scoring average, he also holds the record for the most games with 50 or more points, with 118.

NBA Players with the Highest Career Scoring Averages

Average points per game

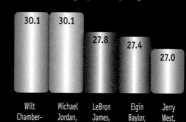

30.1	30.1	27.8	27.4	27.0
Wilt Chamberlain, 1959–1973	Michael Jordan, 1984–1998; 2001–2003	LeBron James, 2003–	Elgin Baylor, 1958–1971	Jerry West, 1960–1974

Michael Jordan

NBA's Highest-Scoring Game

DETROIT PISTONS

On December 13, 1983, the Detroit Pistons beat the Denver Nuggets with a score of 186–184 at McNichols Arena in Denver, Colorado. The game was tied at 145 at the end of regular play, and three overtime periods were needed to determine the winner. During the game, both the Pistons and the Nuggets each had six players who scored in the double figures. Four players scored more than 40 points each, which was an NBA first. The Pistons scored 74 field goals that night, claiming another NBA record that still stands today.

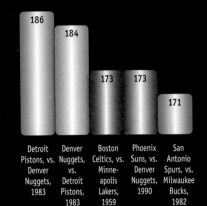

NBA's Highest-Scoring Games
Points scored by a team in one game

186	184	173	173	171
Detroit Pistons, vs. Denver Nuggets, 1983	Denver Nuggets, vs. Detroit Pistons, 1983	Boston Celtics, vs. Minneapolis Lakers, 1959	Phoenix Suns, vs. Denver Nuggets, 1990	San Antonio Spurs, vs. Milwaukee Bucks, 1982

NBA Player with the Highest Salary

TRACY McGRADY

Tracy McGrady was traded to the New York Knicks from the Houston Rockets while making $23.4 million in the last year of his contract. Known as T-Mac, McGrady began his career with the Toronto Raptors in 1997. In 2000, he was traded to the Orlando Magic. He moved to the Rockets in 2004, and later to the Knicks in 2010. McGrady has been on both the All-Star team and the All-NBA team seven times. He also won a gold medal in 2000 at the Sydney Olympics. During 2003 and 2004, McGrady was the NBA Scoring Champion. He has scored 17,534 points during his career, and averages 21.5 points per game.

NBA Players with the Highest Salaries

Annual salary, in millions of US dollars

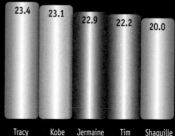

Tracy McGrady	Kobe Bryant	Jermaine O'Neal	Tim Duncan	Shaquille O'Neal
23.4	23.1	22.9	22.2	20.0

NBA Player with the Most Career Points
KAREEM ABDUL-JABBAR

During his highly successful career, Kareem Abdul-Jabbar scored a total of 38,387 points. In 1969, Abdul-Jabbar began his NBA tenure with the Milwaukee Bucks. He was named Rookie of the Year in 1970. The following year he scored 2,596 points and helped the Bucks win the NBA championship. He was traded to the Los Angeles Lakers in 1975, and with his new team, Abdul-Jabbar won the NBA championship in 1980, 1982, 1985, 1987, and 1988. He retired from basketball in 1989 and was inducted into the Basketball Hall of Fame in 1995.

NBA Players with the Most Career Points

Points scored

Kareem Abdul-Jabbar, 1969–1989	Karl Malone, 1985–2004	Michael Jordan, 1984–1998; 2001–2003	Wilt Chamberlain, 1959–1973	Shaquille O'Neal, 1992–
38,387	36,928	32,292	31,419	28,255

WNBA Player with the Most Minutes per Game

KATIE SMITH

Katie Smith spends a lot of time on the court, with an average of 34.7 minutes of play per game. During her career, Smith has played 12,032 minutes in 347 games. Smith began her WNBA career with the Minnesota Lynx in 1999 and was traded to the Detroit Shock in 2005. In 2010, Smith joined the Washington Mystics. In her 11 years as a pro, Smith has scored 5,446 points and grabbed 1,077 rebounds. She has won the WNBA championship with the Shock in 2006 and 2008 and was named to the WNBA All-Star team six times. She also won three Olympic gold medals between 2000 and 2008.

WNBA Players with the Most Minutes per Game

Minutes per game

Katie Smith, 1999–	Tina Thompson, 1997–	Sue Bird, 2002–	Sheryl Swoopes, 1997–2008	Lauren Jackson, 2001–
34.7	34.5	33.5	33.4	32.9

WNBA Player with the Highest Career PPG Average

SEIMONE AUGUSTUS

Minnesota Lynx Seimone Augustus leads the WNBA with an average of 21.2 points per game. Augustus was the first overall draft pick in 2006. The 6-foot (1.8 m) guard from Louisiana State was awarded the Naismith Player of the Year Award in 2005, and went on to win the AP Player of the Year Award in 2006. During her first season with the WNBA, Augustus ranked second in points per game (21.9), field goals made (148), points (744), and field goal attempts (620).

WNBA Players with the Highest Career PPG Averages

Average points per game

Seimone Augustus, 2006–	Cynthia Cooper, 1997–2000	Diana Taurasi, 2004–	Lauren Jackson, 2001–	Cappie Pondexter, 2006–
21.2	21.0	20.3	19.4	19.2

WNBA Player with the Most Career Points
LISA LESLIE

Lisa Leslie—center for the Los Angeles Sparks—has scored 6,263 points in her career. Leslie has a career average of 17.4 points per game. She was named MVP of the WNBA All-Star Games in 1999, 2001, and 2002. Leslie was also a member of the 1996 and 2000 Olympic gold-medal-winning women's basketball teams. In both 2001 and 2002, Leslie led her team to victory in the WNBA championship and was named Finals MVP. Leslie set another record on July 30, 2002, when she became the first player in WNBA history to slam-dunk in a game. Leslie retired at the end of the 2009 season.

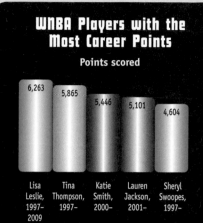

WNBA Players with the Most Career Points

Points scored

Lisa Leslie, 1997–2009	Tina Thompson, 1997–	Katie Smith, 2000–	Lauren Jackson, 2001–	Sheryl Swoopes, 1997–
6,263	5,865	5,446	5,101	4,604

Women's Basketball Team with the Most NCAA Championships

TENNESSEE

The Tennessee Lady Volunteers have won eight NCAA basketball championships. The Lady Vols won their latest championship in 2008. In 1998, they had a perfect record of 39–0, which was the most seasonal wins ever in women's collegiate basketball at the time. In 2004, Tennessee was in the championship but was beaten by the University of Connecticut Huskies. Since 1976, an impressive 14 Lady Vols have been to the Olympics, and 5 Lady Vols have been inducted into the Women's Basketball Hall of Fame in Knoxville, Tennessee.

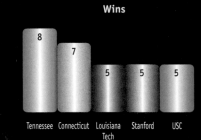

Women's Teams with the Most NCAA Championships
Wins

Tennessee	Connecticut	Louisiana Tech	Stanford	USC
8	7	5	5	5

Men's Basketball Team with the Most NCAA Championships

UCLA

With 11 titles, the University of California, Los Angeles (UCLA) has the most NCAA basketball championship wins. The Bruins won their 11th championship in 1995. The school has won 23 of their last 41 league titles and has been in the NCAA play-offs for 35 of the last 41 years. During the final round of the NCAA championship in 2006, UCLA lost to the Florida Gators with a score of 73–57. Not surprisingly, UCLA has produced some basketball legends, including Kareem Abdul-Jabbar, Reggie Miller, and Baron Davis. For the last 36 years, the Bruins have called Pauley Pavilion home.

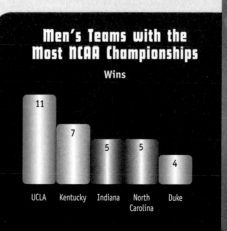

Men's Teams with the Most NCAA Championships
Wins

Team	Wins
UCLA	11
Kentucky	7
Indiana	5
North Carolina	5
Duke	4

NFL Player with the Most Passing Yards

BRETT FAVRE

Quarterback Brett Favre knows how to hit his receivers: He completed 69,329 passing yards during his amazing career. He has a completion rate of 61.6 percent, and has connected for 464 touchdowns. Favre is also the NFL's all-time leader in passing touchdowns (464), completions (5,720), and attempts (9,280). Favre began his career with the Atlanta Falcons in 1991. He was traded to the Green Bay Packers the next season, and played for them until 2007. Favre joined the New York Jets for the season, and was then signed by the Minnesota Vikings for the 2009 season.

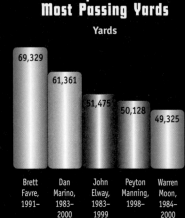

NFL Players with the Most Passing Yards
Yards

Brett Favre, 1991–	Dan Marino, 1983–2000	John Elway, 1983–1999	Peyton Manning, 1998–	Warren Moon, 1984–2000
69,329	61,361	51,475	50,128	49,325

NFL Player with the Highest Career Rushing Total

EMMITT SMITH

Running back Emmitt Smith holds the record for all-time rushing yards with 18,355. Smith began his career with the Dallas Cowboys in 1990 and played with the team until the end of the 2002 season. In 2003, Smith signed a two-year contract with the Arizona Cardinals. Smith also holds the NFL records for the most carries with 4,142 and the most rushing touchdowns with 164. After 15 years in the NFL, Smith retired at the end of the 2004 season.

NFL Players with the Highest Career Rushing Totals

Rushing yards

Emmitt Smith, 1990–2004	Walter Payton, 1975–1987	Barry Sanders, 1989–1999	Curtis Martin, 1995–2007	Jerome Bettis, 1993–2006
18,355	16,726	15,269	14,101	13,662

NFL Player with the Most Career Touchdowns

JERRY RICE

Jerry Rice has scored a record 208 touchdowns. He is widely considered to be one of the greatest wide receivers to ever play in the National Football League. Rice holds a total of 14 NFL records, including career receptions (1,549), receiving yards (22,895), receiving touchdowns (197), consecutive 100-catch seasons (4), most games with 100 receiving yards (73), and many others. He was named NFL Player of the Year twice, *Sports Illustrated* Player of the Year four times, and NFL Offensive Player of the Year once. Rice retired from the NFL in 2005.

NFL Players with the Most Career Touchdowns

Touchdowns scored

208	175	153	147	145
Jerry Rice, 1985–2005	Emmitt Smith, 1990–2004	LaDainian Tomlinson, 2001–	Terrell Owens, 1996–	Marcus Allen, 1982–1996

NFL Player with the Most Single-Season Touchdowns

LADAINIAN TOMLINSON

Running back LaDainian Tomlinson scored 31 touchdowns during the 2006 season. He was also named NFL Most Valuable Player that season for his outstanding performance. During his pro career, he has scored a total of 138 touchdowns. Tomlinson was selected fifth overall in the 2001 draft by the San Diego Chargers but was traded to the New York Jets in 2010. He holds several Chargers records, including 372 attempts (2002), 100 receptions (2003), and 1,815 rushing yards in a season (2006). Tomlinson has also been named to five Pro Bowls.

NFL Players with the Most Single-Season Touchdowns

Touchdowns scored

LaDainian Tomlinson, 2006	Shaun Alexander, 2005	Priest Holmes, 2003	Marshall Faulk, 2000	Emmitt Smith, 1995
31	28	27	26	25

65

NFL Player with the Highest Career Scoring Total

MORTEN ANDERSEN

Morten Andersen led the NFL in scoring with a career total of 2,544 points. He made 565 field goals out of 709 attempts, giving him a 79.9 percent completion rate. He scored 849 extra points out of 859 attempts, resulting in a 98.8 percent success rate. Andersen, a placekicker who began his career in 1982 with the New Orleans Saints, retired in 2008 after playing for the Atlanta Falcons. Known as the Great Dane, partly because of his birthplace of Denmark, Andersen played 382 professional games. His most successful season was in 1995, when he scored 122 points.

NFL Players with the Highest Career Scoring Totals

Points scored

Player	Points scored
Morten Andersen, 1982–2008	2,544
Gary Anderson, 1982–2005	2,434
John Carney, 1988–	2,044
Matt Stover, 1991–	2,004
George Blanda, 1949–1975	2,002

NFL Team with the Most Super Bowl Wins

PITTSBURGH STEELERS

With six championship wins between 1974 and 2009, the Pittsburgh Steelers have won more Super Bowls than any other team in NFL history. The Steelers have also played and won more AFC championship games than any other team in the conference. The Steelers were founded in 1933 and are the fifth-oldest franchise in the league. Twenty-three retired Steelers have been inducted into the Pro Football Hall of Fame, including Franco Harris, Chuck Noll, and Terry Bradshaw.

NFL Teams with the Most Super Bowl Wins

Super Bowls won

Pittsburgh Steelers	Dallas Cowboys	San Francisco 49ers	New England Patriots	New York Giants
6	5	5	3	3

NFL Coach with the Most Wins

DON SHULA

Don Shula led his teams to a remarkable 347 wins during his 33 years as a head coach in the National Football League. When Shula became head coach of the Baltimore Colts in 1963, he became the youngest head coach in football history. He stayed with the team until 1969 and reached the play-offs four times. Shula became the head coach for the Miami Dolphins in 1970 and coached them until 1995. During this time, the Dolphins reached the play-offs 20 times and won at least 10 games a season 21 times. After leading them to Super Bowl wins in 1972 and 1973, Shula became one of only five coaches to win the championship in back-to-back years.

NFL Coaches with the Most Wins
Games won

Don Shula, 1963–1995	George Halas, 1922–1929; 1933–1941; 1946–1955; 1958–1967	Tom Landry, 1960–1988	Curly Lambeau, 1919–1957	Chuck Noel, 1969–1991
347	324	270	229	209

NFL Player with the Highest Salary
PHILIP RIVERS

San Diego Chargers quarterback Philip Rivers earned $25.5 million during the 2009 season. This whopping paycheck breaks down to a $6 million base salary and a $19.5 million signing bonus. That's more than a 174 percent increase from his salary last year. Rivers signed with the Chargers in 2004 after he graduated from North Carolina State. He has 14,951 passing yards and has completed 106 touchdowns. Rivers has a career quarterback rating of 95.8—the second highest of all time in the NFL (behind Steve Young). He was voted into the Pro Bowl in 2006 and 2009.

NFL Players with the Highest Salaries

Annual salary, in millions of US dollars

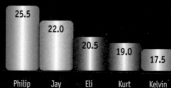

Philip Rivers	Jay Cutler	Eli Manning	Kurt Warner	Kelvin Hayden
25.5	22.0	20.5	19.0	17.5

NFL Team with the Most Consecutive Wins

NEW ENGLAND PATRIOTS

Between 2006 and 2007, the New England Patriots won 19 consecutive games. They ended the 2006 regular season with three wins. During the 2007 regular season, the team won all 16 games—only the fifth team in league history to do so. During this impressive season, the team set an NFL record by scoring 589 points and 75 touchdowns. The Patriots have a winning history, including 10 AFC East championships, 15 NFL play-off appearances, and three Super Bowl wins.

NFL Teams with the Most Consecutive Wins

Consecutive games won

19	18	17	17	16
New England Patriots, 2006–2007	New England Patriots, 2003–2004	Chicago Bears, 1933–1934	Miami Dolphins, 1972–1973	Chicago Bears, 1941–1942

Cyclist with the Most Tour de France Wins

LANCE ARMSTRONG

Lance Armstrong was the first cyclist ever to win seven Tour de France races. He won his first race in 1999, just three years after being diagnosed with cancer. He went on to win the top cycling event for the next six years, retiring after his 2005 victory. Armstrong has received many awards and honors during his career, including being named *Sports Illustrated*'s Sportsman of the Year in 2002. Armstrong also formed the Lance Armstrong Foundation, which supports people recovering from cancer.

Cyclists with the Most Tour de France Wins

Number of wins

Lance Armstrong, USA	Eddy Merckx, Belgium	Jacques Anquetil, France	Bernard Hinault, France	Miguel Indurain, Spain
7	5	5	5	5

71

PGA Golfer with the Lowest Seasonal Average
TIGER WOODS

Tiger Woods was the best on the course in 2009, with a seasonal average of 68.84. Since turning pro in 1996, Woods has played in 253 PGA events and made the cut in about 94 percent of them. He has won 14 professional tournaments, including four Masters wins, three US Open wins, three British Open wins, and four PGA Championship wins. Woods has been named PGA Player of the Year ten times, and he has won the Vardon Trophy eight times. He has earned more than $92.8 million and been the PGA Tour Money Leader nine times. Woods is also the only person who has ever been named *Sports Illustrated*'s Sportsman of the Year more than once.

PGA Golfers with the Lowest Seasonal Averages
Seasonal average in 2009

Tiger Woods	Steve Stricker	David Toms	Tim Clark	Zach Johnson
68.84	69.51	69.74	69.88	69.88

LPGA Golfer with the Lowest Seasonal Average

LORENA OCHOA

Lorena Ochoa had the lowest seasonal average in the LPGA in 2009 with 70.16. She also picked up her fourth consecutive Rolex Player of the Year title. Ochoa, who entered the LPGA in 2003, accomplished several impressive feats in 2006: She won six tournaments and was named Rolex Player of the Year. She earned almost $2.6 million, becoming just the second player to pass $2 million in earnings in a single season. During her short career, Ochoa played in 168 LPGA events and finished in the top three 73 times. She retired from professional golf in April 2010.

LPGA Golfers with the Lowest Seasonal Averages

Seasonal average in 2009

Lorena Ochoa	Jiyai Shin	Cristie Kerr	Ai Miyazato	Yani Tseng
70.16	70.26	70.28	70.33	70.44

LPGA's Highest-Paid Golfer
ANNIKA SORENSTAM

Annika Sorenstam has earned $22.5 million since her LPGA career began in 1994. During this time, she has had 72 career victories, including 9 majors. In 2005, Sorenstam earned her eighth Rolex Player of the Year award—the most in LPGA history. She also became the first player to sweep Rolex Player of the Year honors, the Vare Trophy, and the ADT Official Money List title five times. Sorenstam also earned her fifth consecutive Mizuno Classic title, making her the first golfer in LPGA history to win the same event five consecutive years. Sorenstam retired at the end of the 2008 season.

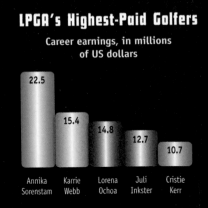

LPGA's Highest-Paid Golfers

Career earnings, in millions of US dollars

Annika Sorenstam	Karrie Webb	Lorena Ochoa	Juli Inkster	Cristie Kerr
22.5	15.4	14.8	12.7	10.7

Golfer with the Most Major Tournament Wins
JACK NICKLAUS

Golfing great Jack Nicklaus has won a total of 18 major championships. His wins include six Masters, five PGAs, four US Opens, and three British Opens. Nicklaus was named PGA Player of the Year five times. He was a member of the winning US Ryder Cup team six times and was an individual World Cup winner a record three times. He was inducted into the World Golf Hall of Fame in 1974, just 12 years after he turned professional. He joined the US Senior PGA Tour in 1990. In addition to playing the game, Nicklaus has designed close to 200 golf courses and has written a number of popular books about the sport.

Golfers with the Most Major Tournament Wins

Major tournament wins

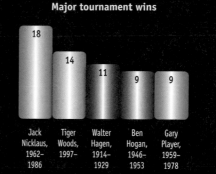

Jack Nicklaus, 1962–1986	Tiger Woods, 1997–	Walter Hagen, 1914–1929	Ben Hogan, 1946–1953	Gary Player, 1959–1978
18	14	11	9	9

MLB Player with the Highest Seasonal Home-Run Total

BARRY BONDS

On October 5, 2001, Barry Bonds smashed Mark McGwire's record for seasonal home runs when he hit his 71st home run in the first inning of a game against the Los Angeles Dodgers. In the third inning, he hit number 72, and two days later he reached 73. Bonds, a left fielder for the San Francisco Giants, has a career total of 762 home runs. He also holds the records for seasonal walks (232) and seasonal on-base percentage (.609). Bonds and his father, hitting coach Bobby Bonds, hold the all-time father-son home-run record with 1,020.

MLB Players with the Highest Seasonal Home-Run Totals

Number of home runs

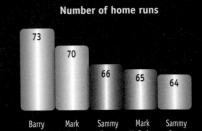

Barry Bonds, 2001	Mark McGwire, 1998	Sammy Sosa, 1998	Mark McGwire, 1999	Sammy Sosa, 2001
73	70	66	65	64

MLB Player with the Most Home Runs

BARRY BONDS

Barry Bonds has hit more home runs than anyone who ever played in the MLB, cracking 762 balls over the wall during his ongoing career. Bonds has hit more than 30 home runs in a season 13 times—another MLB record. During his impressive career, Bonds has won 8 Gold Gloves, 12 Silver Slugger awards, and 13 All-Star awards. Bonds began his career with the Pittsburgh Pirates in 1986; he was transferred to the San Francisco Giants in 1993 and has played for the team since then. He is only one of three players to join the 700 Home Run Club.

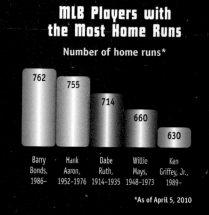

MLB Players with the Most Home Runs

Number of home runs*

Barry Bonds, 1986–	Hank Aaron, 1952–1976	Babe Ruth, 1914–1935	Willie Mays, 1948–1973	Ken Griffey, Jr., 1989–
762	755	714	660	630

*As of April 5, 2010

77

MLB Pitcher with the Most Career Strikeouts

NOLAN RYAN

Nolan Ryan leads Major League Baseball with an incredible 5,714 career strikeouts. In his impressive 28-year career, he played for the New York Mets, the California Angels, the Houston Astros, and the Texas Rangers. The right-handed pitcher from Refugio, Texas, led the American League in strikeouts ten times. In 1989, at the age of 42, Ryan became the oldest pitcher ever to lead the Major Leagues in strikeouts. Ryan set another record in 1991 when he pitched his seventh career no-hitter.

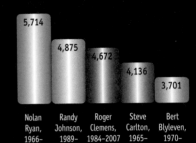

MLB Pitchers with the Most Career Strikeouts

Number of strikeouts

	Number of strikeouts			
5,714	4,875	4,672	4,136	3,701
Nolan Ryan, 1966–1993	Randy Johnson, 1989–2009	Roger Clemens, 1984–2007	Steve Carlton, 1965–1988	Bert Blyleven, 1970–1992

MLB Player with the Most Career Hits

PETE ROSE

Pete Rose belted an amazing 4,256 hits during his 23 years of professional baseball. He got his record-setting hit in 1985, when he was a player-manager for the Cincinnati Reds. By the time Pete Rose retired as a player from Major League Baseball in 1986, he had set several other career records. Rose holds the Major League records for the most career games (3,562), the most times at bat (14,053), and the most seasons with more than 200 hits (10). During his career, he played for the Cincinnati Reds, the Philadelphia Phillies, and the Montreal Expos.

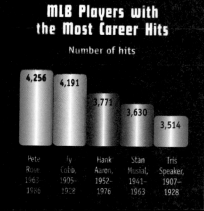

MLB Players with the Most Career Hits

Number of hits

Pete Rose 1963–1986	Ty Cobb, 1905–1928	Hank Aaron, 1952–1976	Stan Musial, 1941–1963	Tris Speaker, 1907–1928
4,256	4,191	3,771	3,630	3,514

MLB Team with the Highest Payroll
NEW YORK YANKEES

The combined 2010 payroll of the New York Yankees totals more than $206 million. Some of the highest-paid players include Alex Rodriguez ($32.0 million), Derek Jeter ($21.0 million), and Mark Teixeira ($20.6). The Yankees have been very successful with their pricey roster, winning 40 American League pennants and 27 World Series. The team also has a new place to showcase its talent—a new Yankee Stadium opened in 2009. The stadium cost $1.5 billion, making it the second-most expensive stadium in the world.

MLB Teams with the Highest Payrolls

Payroll in 2010, in millions of US dollars

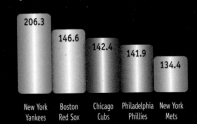

New York Yankees	Boston Red Sox	Chicago Cubs	Philadelphia Phillies	New York Mets
206.3	146.6	142.4	141.9	134.4

MLB Player with the Most Career Runs

RICKEY HENDERSON

During his 25 years in the majors, baseball great Rickey Henderson boasts the most career runs with 2,295. Henderson got his start with the Oakland Athletics in 1979, and went on to play for the Yankees, the Mets, the Mariners, the Red Sox, the Padres, the Dodgers, and the Angels. Henderson won a Gold Glove award in 1981, and the American League MVP award in 1989 and 1990. Henderson is also known as the "Man of Steal" because he holds the MLB record for most stolen bases in a career with 1,406.

MLB Players with the Most Career Runs

Number of career runs

Rickey Henderson, 1979–2003	Ty Cobb, 1905–1928	Barry Bonds, 1986–	Hank Aaron, 1954–1976	Babe Ruth, 1914–1935
2,295	2,245	2,227	2,174	2,174

Yogi Berra

Most MVP Awards in the American League

YOGI BERRA, JOE DIMAGGIO, JIMMIE FOXX, MICKEY MANTLE, & ALEX RODRIGUEZ

With three honors each, Yogi Berra, Joe DiMaggio, Jimmie Foxx, Mickey Mantle, and Alex Rodriguez all hold the record for the Most Valuable Player awards during their professional careers. Berra, DiMaggio, Mantle, and Rodriguez were all New York Yankees. Foxx played for the Athletics, the Cubs, and the Phillies. The player with the biggest gap between wins was DiMaggio, who won his first award in 1939 and his last in 1947. Also nicknamed "Joltin' Joe" and the "Yankee Clipper," DiMaggio began playing in the Major Leagues in 1936. The following year, he led the league in home runs and runs scored. He was inducted into the Baseball Hall of Fame in 1955.

MLB Players with the Most American League MVP Awards

Number of Most Valuable Player (MVP) awards

Yogi Berra, 1946–1963; 1965	Joe DiMaggio, 1936–1951	Jimmie Foxx, 1925–1945	Mickey Mantle, 1951–1968	Alex Rodriguez, 1994–
3	3	3	3	3

Most MVP Awards in the National League

BARRY BONDS

San Francisco Giant Barry Bonds has earned seven Most Valuable Player awards for his amazing achievements in the National League. He received his first two MVP awards in 1990 and 1992 while playing for the Pittsburgh Pirates. The next five awards came while wearing the Giants uniform in 1993, 2001, 2002, 2003, and 2004. Bonds is the first player to win an MVP award three times in consecutive seasons. In fact, Bonds is the only baseball player in history to have won more than three MVP awards.

MLB Players with the Most National League MVP Awards

Number of Most Valuable Player (MVP) awards

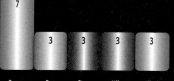

Barry Bonds, 1986–	Roy Campanella, 1948–1957	Stan Musial, 1941–1963	Mike Schmidt, 1972–1989	Albert Pujols, 2001–
7	3	3	3	3

MLB Team with the Most World Series Wins

NEW YORK YANKEES

Between 1923 and 2009, the New York Yankees were the World Series champions a record 27 times. The team picked up their latest win in October of 2009 when they beat the Philadelphia Phillies. The Yankees beat the Phillies four games to two to get their first win in nine years. Since their early days, the team has included some of baseball's greatest players, including Babe Ruth, Lou Gehrig, Yogi Berra, Joe DiMaggio, and Mickey Mantle.

MLB Teams with the Most World Series Wins

Number of wins

NY Yankees	St. Louis Cardinals	Philadelphia/ Kansas City/ Oakland Athletics	Boston Red Sox	Brooklyn/ LA Dodgers
27	10	9	7	6

MLB Pitcher with the Most Cy Young Awards
ROGER CLEMENS

Roger Clemens, a starting pitcher for the Houston Astros, has earned a record seven Cy Young Awards during his career so far. He set a Major League record in April 1986 when he struck out 20 batters in one game. He later tied this record in September 1996. In September 2001, Clemens became the first Major League pitcher to win 20 of his first 21 decisions in one season. In June 2003, he became the first pitcher in more than a decade to win his 300th game. He also struck out his 4,000th batter that year.

MLB Pitchers with the Most Cy Young Awards

Number of Cy Young Awards

Roger Clemens, 1984–	Randy Johnson, 1988–	Steve Carlton, 1965–1988	Greg Maddux, 1986–	Pedro Martinez, 1992–
7	5	4	4	3

MLB Player with the Most At Bats

PETE ROSE

Pete Rose has stood behind the plate for 14,053 at bats—more than any other Major League player. Rose signed with the Cincinnati Reds after graduating from high school in 1963, and played second base. During his impressive career, Rose set several other records, including the most singles in the Major Leagues (3,315), most seasons with 600 or more at bats in the Major Leagues (17), most career doubles in the National League (746), and most career runs in the National League (2,165). He was also named World Series MVP, *Sports Illustrated*'s Sportsman of the Year, and *The Sporting News* Man of the Year.

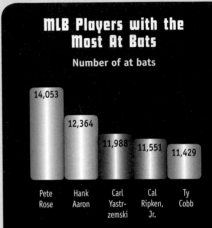

MLB Players with the Most At Bats

Number of at bats

Pete Rose	Hank Aaron	Carl Yastr-zemski	Cal Ripken, Jr.	Ty Cobb
14,053	12,364	11,988	11,551	11,429

MLB Player with the Most Career RBIs

HANK AARON

During his 23 years in the Major Leagues, right-handed Hank Aaron batted in an incredible 2,297 runs. Aaron began his professional career with the Indianapolis Clowns, a team in the Negro American League, in 1952. He was traded to the Milwaukee Braves in 1954 and won the National League batting championship with an average of .328. He was named the league's Most Valuable Player a year later when he led his team to a World Series victory. Aaron retired as a player in 1976 and was inducted into the Baseball Hall of Fame in 1982.

MLB Players with the Most Career RBIs

Number of runs batted in

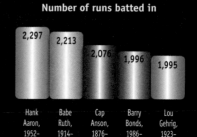

Hank Aaron, 1952–1976	Babe Ruth, 1914–1935	Cap Anson, 1876–1897	Barry Bonds, 1986–	Lou Gehrig, 1923–1939
2,297	2,213	2,076	1,996	1,995

MLB Player with the Most Consecutive Games Played

CAL RIPKEN, JR.

Baltimore Oriole Cal Ripken, Jr., played 2,632 consecutive games from May 30, 1982, to September 20, 1998. The right-handed third baseman also holds the record for the most consecutive innings played: 8,243. In June 1996, Ripken broke the world record for consecutive games with 2,216, surpassing Sachio Kinugasa of Japan. When he played as a shortstop, Ripken set Major League records for most home runs (345) and most extra base hits (855) for his position. He started in the All-Star Game a record 19 times in a row.

MLB Players with the Most Consecutive Games Played

Number of consecutive games played

Cal Ripken, Jr., 1978–2001	Lou Gehrig, 1923–1939	Everett Scott, 1914–1925	Steve Garvey, 1968–1988	Miguel Tejada, 1997–
2,632	2,130	1,307	1,207	1,152

Runner with the Fastest Mile

HICHAM EL GUERROUJ

Moroccan runner Hicham El Guerrouj is super-speedy—he ran a mile in just over 3 minutes and 43 seconds in July 1999 while racing in Rome. He also holds the record for the fastest mile in North America with a time just short of 3 minutes and 50 seconds. El Guerrouj is an Olympian with gold medals in the 1,500-meter and 5,000-meter races. With this accomplishment at the 2004 Athens games, he became the first runner to win both races at the same Olympics in more than 75 years. El Guerrouj returned to the Olympics in 2006 as a torchbearer in Torino, Italy.

Runners with the Fastest Miles

Time, in minutes and seconds

3:43.13	3:43.40	3:44.39	3:44.60	3:44.90
Hicham El Guerrouj, Morocco	Noah Ngeny, Kenya	Noureddine Morceli, Algeria	Hicham El Guerrouj, Morocco	Hicham El Guerrouj, Morocco

Top-Earning Female Tennis Player
SERENA WILLIAMS

Serena Williams has earned $30.4 million since she began playing professional tennis in 1995. During her amazing career, Williams has won 36 singles championships and 17 doubles championships, as well as two gold medals in the 2000 and 2008 Olympics. She has also won all four of the Grand Slam championships. Williams has won many impressive awards, including AP's Female Athlete of the Year, the BBC's Sports Personality of the Year, and two Espy Awards.

Top-Earning Female Tennis Players

Career earnings, in millions of US dollars

30.4	26.1	22.1	21.8	21.6
Serena Williams, 1995–	Venus Williams, 1994–	Lindsay Davenport, 1993–	Steffi Graf, 1982–1999	Martina Navratilova, 1975–1994

Top-Earning Male Tennis Player

ROGER FEDERER

Tennis great Roger Federer has earned more than $55.4 million since his career began in 1998. He has won 63 singles titles and eight doubles titles, including 16 Grand Slams. His major victories include four Australian Opens, one French Open, six Wimbledon titles, and five US Opens. From February 2, 2004, to August 17, 2008, Federer was ranked first in the world for 237 consecutive weeks. He is also the only player in history to win five consecutive titles at two different Grand Slam tournaments (Wimbledon and US Open).

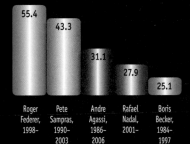

Top-Earning Male Tennis Players

Career earnings, in millions of US dollars

Roger Federer, 1998–	Pete Sampras, 1990–2003	Andre Agassi, 1986–2006	Rafael Nadal, 2001–	Boris Becker, 1984–1997
55.4	43.3	31.1	27.9	25.1

Woman with the Most Grand Slam Singles Titles

MARGARET COURT SMITH

Margaret Court Smith won 24 Grand Slam singles titles between 1960 and 1975. She is the only woman ever to win the French, British, US, and Australian titles during one year in both the singles and doubles competitions. She was only the second woman to win all four singles titles in the same year. During her amazing career, she won a total of 66 Grand Slam championships—more than any other woman. Court was the world's top-seeded female player from 1962 to 1965, 1969 to 1970, and 1973. She was inducted into the International Tennis Hall of Fame in 1979.

Women with the Most Grand Slam Singles Titles

Number of titles won

Margaret Court Smith, 1960–1975	Steffi Graf, 1987–1999	Helen Wills-Moody, 1923–1938	Chris Evert-Lloyd, 1974–1986	Martina Navratilova, 1975–1995
24	22	19	18	18

Man with the Most Grand Slam Singles Titles

ROGER FEDERER

Swiss tennis great Roger Federer has won a record 16 Grand Slam championship titles and earned more than $55.4 million since he turned pro in 1998. He has four Australian Open wins, one French Open win, six Wimbledon wins, and five US Open wins. Federer is also one of only two players to win the Golden Slam—winning all four Grand Slam championships and an Olympic gold medal in the same year (2008). Federer ended 2009 as the ATP World Tour Champion for the fifth time in six years.

Men with the Most Grand Slam Singles Titles

Number of titles won

Roger Federer, 2003–	Pete Sampras, 1990–2002	Roy Emerson, 1961–1967	Bjorn Borg, 1974–1981	Rod Laver, 1960–1969
16	14	12	12	11

Country with the Most Summer Olympic Medals

UNITED STATES

The United States has won 2,301 medals during the Summer Olympics since officials first began recording the victories in 1896. The medal count breaks down to 932 gold, 730 silver, and 639 bronze. In fact, the United States has more gold medals than the next two highest countries combined. Some summer sports, including men's and women's basketball, have been consistently dominated by Americans throughout the years. The United States also excels in swimming and gymnastics.

Countries with the Most Summer Olympic Medals

Number of medals won

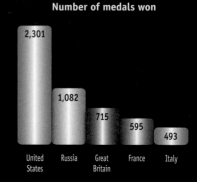

United States	Russia	Great Britain	France	Italy
2,301	1,082	715	595	493

Country with the Most Winter Olympic Medals

NORWAY

With 303 Olympic medals, Norway leads the world in the winter competition since tallies were first kept in 1924. Norway's medal count consists of 107 gold, 106 silver, and 90 bronze. In fact, several Nordic athletes hold the record for the most medals won in the Winter Olympics—Bjorn Daehlie holds 12 medals in cross country and Ole Einar Bjoerndalen has 9 in the biathlon. The country's chilly climate and mountainous terrain create a perfect place to practice many of the competition's most popular sports, including skiing, bobsled, and snowboarding.

Countries with the Most Winter Olympic Medals

Number of medals won

Norway	United States	Russia	Austria	Germany
303	253	209	201	196

Woman with the Most World Figure Skating Championship Wins

SONJA HENIE

Sonja Henie was the queen of the ice, winning ten World Figure Skating Championships between 1927 and 1936. She also won six European Championships and three Olympic gold medals during her distinguished career. Born in Norway, Henie was one of the first female skaters to add dance choreography and flashy costumes to her routine. After her final championship in 1936, Henie went to Hollywood and became one of the highest-paid actresses of her time.

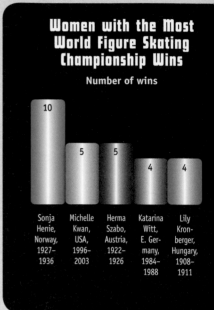

Women with the Most World Figure Skating Championship Wins

Number of wins

10	5	5	4	4
Sonja Henie, Norway, 1927–1936	Michelle Kwan, USA, 1996–2003	Herma Szabo, Austria, 1922–1926	Katarina Witt, E. Germany, 1984–1988	Lily Kronberger, Hungary, 1908–1911

Man with the Most World Figure Skating Championship Wins

ULRICH SALCHOW

Swedish figure skater Ulrich Salchow won the World Figure Skating Championships ten times between 1901 and 1911. He also took second place in three other World Championships. Salchow was the first person to land a jump in competition in which he started on the back inside edge of one skate and landed on the back outside edge of the other skate. It was named the Salchow jump in his honor. He also won the first Olympic medal awarded in figure skating when he took the gold at the 1908 games in London.

Men with the Most World Figure Skating Championship Wins

Number of wins

Ulrich Salchow, Sweden, 1901–1911	Karl Schäfer, Austria, 1930–1936	Richard Button, USA, 1948–1952	Kurt Browning, Canada, 1989–1993	Scott Hamilton, USA, 1981–1984
10	7	5	4	4

Women's Soccer Team with the Most World Cup Points

USA

The USA women's soccer team has accumulated 14 points during World Cup competition. The Fédération Internationale de Football Association (FIFA) awards 4 points for a win, 3 points for runner-up, 2 points for third place, and 1 point for fourth. The United States won the Cup in 1991 and 1999. They came in third place in 1995, 2003, and 2007. Some of the star players on the US team at the time of these wins included Mia Hamm, Julie Foudy, Brandi Chastain, Kristine Lilly, and Briana Scurry.

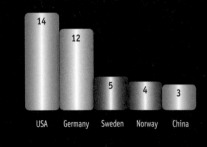

Women's Soccer Teams with the Most World Cup Points

Total number of World Cup points

USA	Germany	Sweden	Norway	China
14	12	5	4	3

Soccer Player with the Highest Salary

LIONEL MESSI

Lionel Messi earns a whopping $39.6 million a year for playing striker/winger for La Liga's Barcelona team. Messi has won the Ballon d'Or and been named the FIFA World Player of the Year. During the 2004 season, the 17-year-old Messi made history by becoming the youngest person to score a goal in La Liga. Two years later, he became the youngest Argentinean to play in the FIFA World Cup. In 2008, Messi competed at the Olympics in Beijing and brought home the gold medal with the Argentinean team. He has scored 13 goals in international competition.

Soccer Players with the Highest Salaries

Annual salary, in millions of US dollars

Lionel Messi, Barcelona	David Beckham, LA Galaxy	Cristiano Ronaldo, Real Madrid	Kaka, Real Madrid	Thierry Henry, Barcelona
39.6	36.5	36.0	22.6	21.7

Woman with the Most CAPS

KRISTINE LILLY

With a total of 342, Kristine Lilly holds the world record for the most CAPS, or international games played. This is the highest number of CAPS in both the men's and women's international soccer organizations. Lilly has played more than 23,500 minutes—that's 392 hours—for the US national team. In 2004, Lilly scored her 100th international goal, becoming one of only five women to ever accomplish that feat. In 2005, Lilly was named US Soccer's Female Athlete of the Year.

Women with the Most CAPS

Number of career CAPS

Kristine Lilly, USA, 1987–	Mia Hamm, USA, 1987– 2004	Julie Foudy, USA, 1988– 2004	Joy Fawcett, USA, 1987– 2004	Christie Rampone, USA, 1997–
342	275	271	239	216

Man with the Most CAPS
MOHAMED AL-DEAYEA

Saudi Arabian soccer great Mohamed Al-Deayea has the most CAPS, or international games, with 181. Al-Deayea began his professional career as a goalie with the Saudi team Al-Ta'ee in 1991 and played there for nine years. In 2000, he became the captain of Al-Hilal. While playing as a part of the Saudi national team, Al-Deayea reached the World Cup three times between 1994 and 2002. He was placed on the 2006 World Cup team but did not play in any games. At the end of the competition, Al-Deayea announced his retirement.

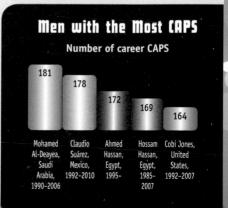

Men with the Most CAPS
Number of career CAPS

Mohamed Al-Deayea, Saudi Arabia, 1990–2006	Claudio Suárez, Mexico, 1992–2010	Ahmed Hassan, Egypt, 1995–	Hossam Hassan, Egypt, 1985–2007	Cobi Jones, United States, 1992–2007
181	178	172	169	164

Country with the Most World Cup Points

GERMANY

Germany has accumulated a total of 31 points during World Cup soccer competition. A win is worth 4 points, runner-up is worth 3 points, third place is worth 2 points, and fourth place is worth 1 point. Germany won the World Cup four times between 1954 and 1990. Most recently, Germany earned 2 points for a third-place finish in 2006. The World Cup is organized by the Fédération Internationale de Football Association (FIFA) and is played every four years.

Countries with the Most World Cup Points

Total number of points

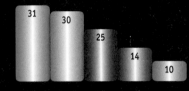

Germany/ W. Germany, 1954– 2006	Brazil, 1958– 2002	Italy, 1934– 2006	Argentina, 1978– 1986	Uruguay, 1930– 1950
31	30	25	14	10

Driver with the Most Formula One Wins

MICHAEL SCHUMACHER

Race-car driver Michael Schumacher won 91 Formula One races in his professional career, which began in 1991. Out of the 250 races he competed in, he reached the podium 154 times. In 2002, Schumacher became the only Formula One driver to have a podium finish in each race in which he competed that season. He won seven world championships between 1994 and 2004. Schumacher, who was born in Germany, began his career with Benetton but later switched to Ferrari. He retired from racing in 2006.

Drivers with the Most Formula One Wins

Number of wins

Michael Schumacher	Alain Prost	Ayrton Senna	Nigel Mansell	Jackie Stewart
91	51	41	31	27

Driver with the Fastest Daytona 500 Win

BUDDY BAKER

Race-car legend Buddy Baker dominated the competition at the 1980 Daytona 500 with an average speed of over 177 miles (285 km) per hour. It was the first Daytona 500 race run under three hours. Baker had a history of speed before this race—he became the first driver to race more than 200 miles (322 km) per hour on a closed course in 1970. During his amazing career, Baker competed in 688 Winston Cup races—he won 19 of them and finished in the top five in 198 others. He also won more than $3.6 million. He was inducted into the International Motorsports Hall of Fame in 1997.

Drivers with the Fastest Daytona 500 Wins

Average speed, in miles (kilometers) per hour

177.60 (285.82)	176.26 (283.66)	172.71 (277.95)	172.26 (277.23)	169.65 (273.03)
Buddy Baker, 1980	Bill Elliott, 1987	Dale Earnhardt, 1998	Bill Elliott, 1985	Richard Petty, 1981

Driver with the Fastest Indianapolis 500 Win
ARIE LUYENDYK

In 1990, race-car driver Arie Luyendyk won the Indianapolis 500 with an average speed of almost 186 miles (299 km) per hour—the fastest average speed ever recorded in the history of the race. This was the first Indy 500 race for Luyendyk, and he drove a Lola/Chevy Indy V8 as part of the Shierson Racing team. In 1997, Luyendyk had another Indy 500 victory with an average speed of 146 miles (235 km) per hour. He also holds the record for the fastest Indy 500 practice lap at a speed of 239 miles (385 km) per hour.

Drivers with the Fastest Indianapolis 500 Wins
Average speed, in miles (kilometers) per hour

Arie Luyendyk, 1990	Rick Mears, 1991	Bobby Rahal, 1986	Juan-Pablo Montoya, 2000	Emerson Fittipaldi, 1989
185.98 (299.30)	176.45 (283.98)	170.72 (274.75)	167.61 (269.73)	167.58 (269.73)

105

NASCAR Driver with the Highest Career Earnings

JEFF GORDON

Jeff Gordon has earned more than $111 million since he began racing in 1991. In fact, he was the first driver in history to earn more than $50 million. To date, Gordon has won 4 Winston Cup titles, 3 Daytona 500 titles, and 73 NASCAR Cup victories. His first Daytona 500 win in 1997 came when he was just 25 years old, making him the race's youngest winner. Gordon has 82 career NASCAR victories, placing him sixth on the all-time wins list. He has raced for Hendrick Motorsports since 1992, and is part owner in the business.

NASCAR Drivers with the Highest Career Earnings

Career earnings, in millions of US dollars

Jeff Gordon	Jimmie Johnson	Tony Stewart	Mark Martin	Matt Kenseth
111.4	91.6	83.3	77.4	68.1

Rider with the Most Superbike Rank Points
BEN SPIES

Ben Spies earned a total of 462 points during the 2009 Superbike World Championship season. During his rookie season, Spies won 14 races and reached the podium 17 times as a member of the Yamaha Italia team. On May 30, 2009, Spies earned his seventh consecutive pole position, setting a record for the most consecutive poles in a season. He now races for the Yamaha Monster Tech 3 team and wears number 11. Spies turned pro in 2000 and raced in the AMA Superbike Championship for eight years. There he won the championship each year between 2006 and 2008.

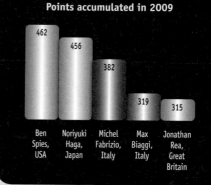

Riders with the Most Superbike Rank Points
Points accumulated in 2009

Ben Spies, USA	Noriyuki Haga, Japan	Michel Fabrizio, Italy	Max Biaggi, Italy	Jonathan Rea, Great Britain
462	456	382	319	315

Rider with the Most Motocross World Titles
STEFAN EVERTS

Stefan Everts is the king of motocross with a total of ten world titles. He won twice on a 500cc bike, seven more times on a 250cc bike, and once on a 125cc bike. During his 18-year career, he had 101 Grand Prix victories. Everts was named Belgium Sportsman of the Year five times. He retired after his final world title in 2006 and is now a consultant and coach for the riders who compete for the KTM racing team.

Riders with the Most Motocross World Titles
Number of wins

Stefan Everts, Belgium	Joel Robert, Belgium	Roger de Coster, Belgium	Eric Geboers, Belgium	Georges Jobe, Belgium
10	6	5	5	5

Jockey with the Most Triple Crown Wins
EDDIE ARCARO

Between 1938 and 1961, jockey Eddie Arcaro won a total of 17 Triple Crown races. Nicknamed "the Master," Arcaro won the Kentucky Derby five times, the Preakness six times, and the Belmont six times. He holds the record for the most Preakness wins, and is tied for the most Kentucky Derby and Belmont wins. He was also horse racing's top money winner six times between 1940 and 1955. During his career, Arcaro competed in 24,092 races and won 4,779 of them.

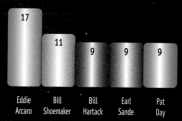

Jockeys with the Most Triple Crown Wins

Number of wins

Eddie Arcaro	Bill Shoemaker	Bill Hartack	Earl Sande	Pat Day
17	11	9	9	9

NHL Team with the Most Stanley Cup Wins
MONTREAL CANADIENS

The Montreal Canadiens won an amazing 24 Stanley Cup victories between 1916 and 1993. That's almost one-quarter of all the Stanley Cup championships ever played. The team plays at Montreal's Molson Centre. The Canadiens were created in December 1909 by J. Ambrose O'Brien to play for the National Hockey Association (NHA). They eventually made the transition into the National Hockey League. Over the years, the Canadiens have included such great players as Maurice Richard, George Hainsworth, Jacques Lemaire, Saku Koivu, and Emile Bouchard.

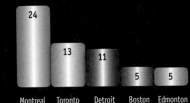

NHL Teams with the Most Stanley Cup Wins
Number of Stanley Cup wins

Montreal Canadiens	Toronto Maple Leafs	Detroit Red Wings	Boston Bruins	Edmonton Oilers
24	13	11	5	5

NHL Player with the Most Career Points
WAYNE GRETZKY

Wayne Gretzky scored an unbelievable 2,857 points and 894 goals during his 20-year career. Gretzky was the first person in the NHL to average more than two points per game. Many people consider Canadian-born Gretzky to be the greatest player in the history of the National Hockey League. In fact, he is called "the Great One." He officially retired from the sport in 1999 and was inducted into the Hockey Hall of Fame that same year. After his final game, the NHL retired his jersey number (99). In 2005, Gretzky became the head coach of the Phoenix Coyotes.

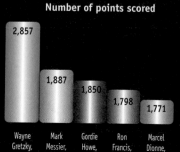

NHL Players with the Most Career Points

Number of points scored

Wayne Gretzky, 1979–1999	Mark Messier, 1979–2004	Gordie Howe, 1954–1980	Ron Francis, 1981–2004	Marcel Dionne, 1971–1990
2,857	1,887	1,850	1,798	1,771

NHL Goalie with the Most Career Wins

MARTIN BRODEUR

Not much gets by goalie Martin Brodeur—he's won 599 games since he was drafted by the New Jersey Devils in 1990. Still playing with the Devils, Brodeur has helped the team win three Stanley Cup championships. He is also the only goalie in NHL history to complete seven seasons with 40 or more wins. Brodeur has been an NHL All-Star ten times, and has received the Vezina Trophy and the Jennings Trophy four times each. He also ranks second in the league in regular-season shutouts.

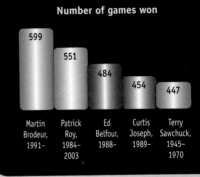

NHL Goalies with the Most Career Wins

Number of games won

599	551	484	454	447
Martin Brodeur, 1991–	Patrick Roy, 1984–2003	Ed Belfour, 1988–	Curtis Joseph, 1989–	Terry Sawchuck, 1945–1970

Most Valuable Hockey Team

TORONTO MAPLE LEAFS

The Toronto Maple Leafs are worth an astounding $470 million, making them the most valuable hockey team in the world. This value is determined by assigning a monetary value to each of the team's players, based on their skills, performance, and contract value. Formerly known as the Toronto Arenas, the team was formed in 1917. Ten years later, the team changed to its current name. The Leafs won 13 Stanley Cups between 1918 and 1967. Some of the most famous players associated with the team include Turk Broda, Tim Horton, Syl Apps, Darryl Sittler, and Ed Belfour. The team's home ice is at the Air Canada Centre.

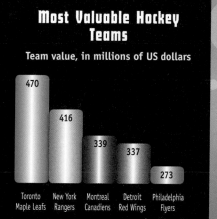

Most Valuable Hockey Teams

Team value, in millions of US dollars

Toronto Maple Leafs	New York Rangers	Montreal Canadiens	Detroit Red Wings	Philadelphia Flyers
470	416	339	337	273

Skateboarder with the Most X Game Gold Medals

TONY HAWK

American Tony Hawk won ten gold medals for skateboarding in the Extreme Games between 1995 and 2002. All his medals came in vertical competition, meaning that the riders compete on a vert ramp similar to a half-pipe. Hawk is most famous for nailing the 900—completing 2.5 rotations in the air before landing back on the ramp. He has also invented many skateboarding tricks, including the McHawk, the Madonna, and the Stalefish. Although Hawk is retired from professional skateboarding, he is still active in several businesses, including video game consulting, film production, and clothing design.

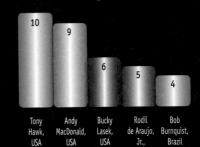

Skateboarders with the Most X Game Gold Medals

Number of gold medals won

Tony Hawk, USA	Andy MacDonald, USA	Bucky Lasek, USA	Rodil de Araujo, Jr., Brazil	Bob Burnquist, Brazil
10	9	6	5	4

Athlete with the Most X Game Medals

DAVE MIRRA

Dave Mirra has won 21 medals—14 gold, 4 silver, and 3 bronze—in X Game competition. He has medaled in every X Game since he entered the games in 1995. All of Mirra's medals have come in BMX competition, where he performs tricks such as double backflips, front flips, triple tail whips, and backflip drop-ins. In 2006, Mirra formed his own bike company named Mirraco, and he now competes for the company with other top BMX riders. That same year marked Mirra's first absence from the X Games because of injury.

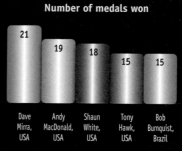

Athletes with the Most X Game Medals

Number of medals won

Dave Mirra, USA	Andy MacDonald, USA	Shaun White, USA	Tony Hawk, USA	Bob Burnquist, Brazil
21	19	18	15	15

Snowboarder with the Most World Championship Medals

NICOLAS HUET

Nicolas Huet has won five championship medals while competing as a snowboarder with the Fédération Internationale de Ski (FIS). Huet's medals include two golds, one silver, and two bronzes. Huet's first medal came in 1999 when he won gold in Germany, and his most recent medals came in 2005 when he won a silver and a bronze in Canada. His medals were earned on the parallel slalom and the parallel giant slalom. Nicknamed Nico, Huet spends his time golfing and surfing when he's not on the slopes.

Snowboarders with the Most World Championship Medals

Number of medals won

Nicolas Huet, France	Antti Autti, Finland	Jasey-Jay Anderson, Canada	Mike Jacoby, USA	Helmut Pramstaller, Austria
5	4	4	3	3

SCIENCE RECORDS

Video Games • Internet • Computers
Vehicles • Technology

Bestselling Family Video Game

WII SPORTS RESORT

Wii Sports Resort sold more than 7.57 million copies worldwide in 2009. The game sold more than 1 million copies in the first week after it debuted in the United States in July 2009. The game features 12 different sports that are set at a beach resort called Wuhu Island. Some of the sports include wakeboarding, Frisbee, archery, table tennis, golf, canoeing, basketball, swordplay, and cycling. Most of these games can accommodate between one and four players. This new Wii game also incorporates MotionPlus, a technology that helps the player perform movements with more accuracy.

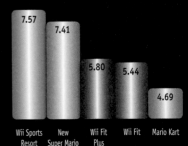

Bestselling Family Video Games of 2009

Units sold in 2009, in millions

Wii Sports Resort	New Super Mario Bros	Wii Fit Plus	Wii Fit	Mario Kart
7.57	7.41	5.80	5.44	4.69

Country that Spends the Most on Video Games
UNITED KINGDOM

Each person in the United Kingdom spends approximately $67 on video games each year. That's a total of about $4.1 billion! This is an increase of more than 40 percent in the last two years. Gaming is quickly becoming a favorite pastime in the UK—sales of video games far surpassed sales of movie and theater tickets combined. This increase is partially due to a renewed interest in bringing entertainment into the home. Media stores are even rearranging their displays, featuring video games in the front of the stores and moving music and DVDs to the back. Some of the more popular games in the region include FIFA 09 and Wii Sports.

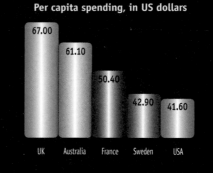

Countries that Spend the Most on Video Games

Per capita spending, in US dollars

UK	Australia	France	Sweden	USA
67.00	61.10	50.40	42.90	41.60

Most-Visited Website

GOOGLE

The Web search engine Google has 139.5 million unique users each month. That's the equivalent of half the United States' population logging on to the site! Google is the world's largest online index of websites. In addition, Google offers e-mail, maps, news, and finance sites. Google was founded in 1998 by Stanford University students Larry Page and Sergey Brin. A "googol" is a 1 followed by 100 zeros, and the site was named after the term to indicate its mission to organize the virtually infinite amount of information on the Web.

Most-Visited Websites

Number of unique users each month, in millions

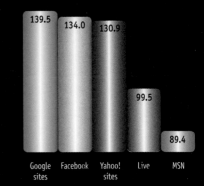

Google sites	Facebook	Yahoo! sites	Live	MSN
139.5	134.0	130.9	99.5	89.4

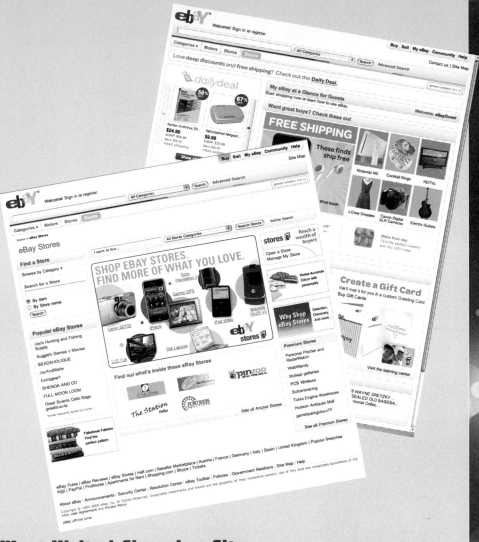

Most-Visited Shopping Site

EBAY

When online shoppers are looking to spend money, the majority check eBay first. With 71.8 million visitors each month, eBay truly is the World's Online Marketplace. The company was founded in 1995, and the online auction and shopping website attracts sellers and bidders from all over the world. Each year, millions of items—including spectacular treasures, unusual services, and even worthless junk—trade hands. Some of the most expensive sales include a Grumman Gulfstream II jet for $4.9 million and a 1909 Honus Wagner baseball card for $1.65 million.

Most-Visited Shopping Sites

Number of unique users each month, in millions

- eBay.com — 71.8
- Amazon.com — 68.1
- Apple.com — 56.6
- Craigslist.com — 47.1
- Target.com — 34.8

Most-Visited Social Network Site

FACEBOOK

The social site Facebook has more than 134 million unique visitors each month. Facebook was created by Mark Zuckerberg in 2004 as a network site for Harvard University students to chat with one another, send messages, and post updates on their walls. It was a huge hit, and was up and running at more than 30 other universities within four months. In 2007, Facebook took off with mainstream users and was registering about 1 million new users a week. Today, most users sign on every day, and spend an average of 19 minutes a day socializing.

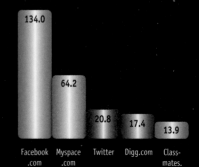

Most-Visited Social Network Sites

Unique visits per month, in millions

Facebook.com	Myspace.com	Twitter	Digg.com	Classmates.com
134.0	64.2	20.8	17.4	13.9

Most-Visited Newspaper Website

NYTIMES.COM

Each month, approximately 19.5 million people log on to check out the latest happenings around the world on the *New York Times* website. The site offers everything found in the print edition, including US and world news, sports, science, arts, travel, and classified sections. The online readers for the *Times* increased about 6 percent from the previous year, and online newspapers in general increased readership by about 27 percent. Because Internet access is so readily available at home, work, schools, libraries, and even phones, online news is often faster and easier to obtain than the printed version.

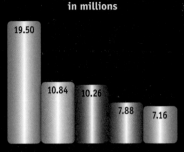

Most-Visited Newspaper Websites

Average visitors per month, in millions

Website	Visitors
Nytimes.com	19.50
Usatoday.com	10.84
Washingtonpost.com	10.26
Latimes.com	7.88
Wallstreet journal.com	7.16

Most-Used E-mail Service
YAHOO! MAIL

Yahoo! Mail has more than 106,600 unique visitors each month—more than the next two most popular e-mail services combined—and more than 274 million users worldwide. Some popular features that the e-mail service includes are unlimited e-mail storage, instant and text messaging from mailboxes, and advanced protection from spam and viruses. The mail service, which is part of the bigger Yahoo! company, began in 1996. Founders David Filo and Jerry Yang created Yahoo! while they were students at Stanford University.

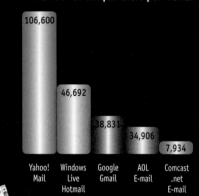

Most-Used E-mail Services

Number of unique users per month

Yahoo! Mail	Windows Live Hotmail	Google Gmail	AOL E-mail	Comcast .net E-mail
106,600	46,692	38,831	34,906	7,934

Country with the Most Websites

UNITED STATES

The United States has the most sites on the World Wide Web with 383 million. That's more than half of the 665 million sites worldwide that make up the Internet today. There are currently about 5,000 times more websites running today than there were on the Web just ten years ago. Website production has increased at this incredible rate because sites have become so much easier to create. Bloggers and small business owners account for the largest percentage of new websites.

Countries with the Most Websites

Number of websites, in millions

USA	383.0
Japan	47.2
Germany	23.7
Italy	22.1
Brazil	15.9

Country with the Highest Internet Usage

ICELAND

Iceland has the world's highest percentage of Internet users, with more than 93 percent of the country logging on to surf the Web. That means about 295,400 people in the small European country have Internet access, and 97,900 are broadband subscribers. In comparison, only about 52 percent of the population in Europe as a whole goes online. Icelandic people mainly use the Internet to find information and to communicate, with about 36 percent of users also shopping online. Iceland has about 20 Internet providers, and subscribers pay approximately $60 a month for service.

Countries with the Highest Internet Usage

Percentage of population

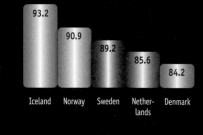

Iceland	Norway	Sweden	Nether-lands	Denmark
93.2	90.9	89.2	85.6	84.2

Country with the Most Internet Users

CHINA

China dominates the world in Internet usage, with 384 million people—or about one-third of the country—browsing the World Wide Web under government censorship. This is a huge increase of about 29 percent from last year. About 233 million Internet users browse from their cell phones. These phone surfers account for much of the increase in Internet users. Internet usage in rural areas is also growing, increasing by about 26 percent last year. Some Internet activities that are becoming increasingly popular in China include banking and booking travel.

Countries with the Most Internet Users

Users, in millions

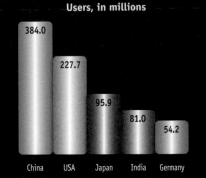

China	USA	Japan	India	Germany
384.0	227.7	95.9	81.0	54.2

127

Country with the Most Personal Computers

UNITED STATES

Throughout the United States, there are a total of 274.1 million personal computers in use. This is more than 22 percent of the world's total personal computer usage. In 2008, 86 percent of the population used a personal computer. It's estimated that the United States will have more computers in use than it will have people by 2013. The United States is one of only two countries that has more PCs in use than it has cell phone subscribers. The total number of personal computers in use worldwide totals 1.2 billion units.

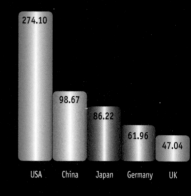

Countries with the Most Personal Computers

Personal computers in use, in millions

USA	China	Japan	Germany	UK
274.10	98.67	86.22	61.96	47.04

Fastest Passenger Train
MAGLEV

The superspeedy MagLev train in China carries passengers from Pudong financial district to Pudong International Airport at an average speed of 267 miles (427 km) per hour. The 8-minute train ride replaces a 45-minute car trip. A one-way ticket costs about $7.30. The MagLev, which is short for "magnetic levitation," actually floats in the air just above the track. Tiny magnets are used to suspend the train, and larger ones are used to pull it forward. The German-built train began commercial operation in 2004.

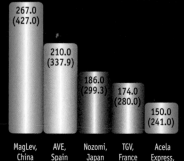

Fastest Passenger Trains

Average speed, in miles (kilometers) per hour

MagLev, China	267.0 (427.0)
AVE, Spain	210.0 (337.9)
Nozomi, Japan	186.0 (299.3)
TGV, France	174.0 (280.0)
Acela Express, USA	150.0 (241.0)

Smallest Car

PEEL P50

The Peel P50 is the smallest production car ever made, measuring just 4.25 feet (1.3 m) long. That's not much longer than the average adult bicycle! The Peel P50 was produced in the Isle of Man between 1962 and 1965, and only 46 cars were made. It is just big enough to hold one adult and one bag. The Peel P50 has three wheels, one door, one windshield wiper, and one headlight, and was available in red, white, or blue. The microcar weighs just 130 pounds (58.9 kg) and measures about 4 feet (1.2 m) tall. With its three-speed manual transmission, it can reach a top speed of 38 miles (61 km) an hour. However, it cannot go in reverse.

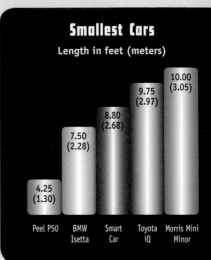

Smallest Cars

Length in feet (meters)

Peel P50	BMW Isetta	Smart Car	Toyota iQ	Morris Mini Minor
4.25 (1.30)	7.50 (2.28)	8.80 (2.68)	9.75 (2.97)	10.00 (3.05)

Fastest Land Vehicle

THRUST SSC

The Thrust SSC, which stands for Supersonic Car, reached a speed of 763 miles (1,228 km) per hour on October 15, 1997. At that speed, a car could make it from San Francisco to New York City in less than four hours. The Thrust SSC is propelled by two jet engines capable of 110,000 horsepower. It has the same power as 1,000 Ford Escorts or 145 Formula One race cars. The Thrust SSC runs on jet fuel, using about five gallons (19 L) per second. It takes only approximately five seconds for this supersonic car to reach its top speed. It is 54 feet (16.5 m) long and weighs seven tons (6.4 t).

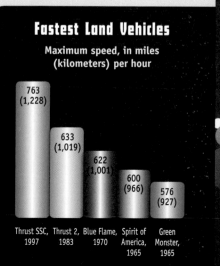

Fastest Land Vehicles

Maximum speed, in miles (kilometers) per hour

763 (1,228)	633 (1,019)	622 (1,001)	600 (966)	576 (927)
Thrust SSC, 1997	Thrust 2, 1983	Blue Flame, 1970	Spirit of America, 1965	Green Monster, 1965

Fastest Production Car

SSC ULTIMATE AERO

The superspeedy SSC Ultimate Aero can reach a top speed of 257 miles (414 km) per hour! At that rate, person could drive from Boston to Los Angeles in just 11.5 hours. The Aero can accelerate from 0 to 60 miles per hour in just 2.78 seconds, and cover a quarter mile in just 9.9 seconds. The Aero is powered by a twin turbo V-8 engine producing 1,183 horsepower. The SSC Ultimate Aero is built by Shelby Super Cars, and the design took seven years to perfect.

Fastest Production Cars

Maximum speed, in miles (kilometers) per hour

SSC Ultimate Aero	Bugatti Veyron	Koenigsegg CCXR	Saleen S7 Twin Turbo	McLaren F1
257 (414)	253 (407)	250 (402)	248 (399)	240 (386)

Biggest Monster Truck

BIGFOOT 5

The Bigfoot 5 truly is a monster—it measures 15.4 feet (4.7 m) high! That's about three times the height of an average car. Bigfoot 5 has 10-foot (3 m) Firestone Tundra tires, each weighing 2,400 pounds (1,088 kg), giving the truck a total weight of about 38,000 pounds (17,236 kg). The giant wheels were from an arctic snow train operated in Alaska by the US Army in the 1950s. This modified 1996 Ford F250 pickup truck is owned by Bob Chandler of St. Louis, Missouri. The great weight of this monster truck makes it too large to race.

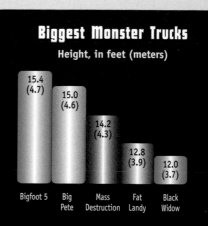

Biggest Monster Trucks
Height, in feet (meters)

Bigfoot 5	Big Pete	Mass Destruction	Fat Landy	Black Widow
15.4 (4.7)	15.0 (4.6)	14.2 (4.3)	12.8 (3.9)	12.0 (3.7)

Largest Cruise Ships

OASIS OF THE SEAS & ALLURE OF THE SEAS

Royal Caribbean's sister cruise ships—*Oasis of the Seas* and *Allure of the Seas*—weigh in at 225,282 gross tons (228,897 t) each! These giant ships are more like floating cities with seven different themed neighborhoods: Central Park, Boardwalk, Royal Promenade, Pool and Sports Zone, Vitality at Sea Spa and Fitness Center, Entertainment Place, and Youth Zone. *Oasis of the Seas* and *Allure of the Seas* each span 16 decks and include more than 20 eateries, 3 pools, a water park, and a zip-line ride. Both ships have 2,700 staterooms and can accommodate a whopping 5,400 guests.

Largest Cruise Ships
Weight, in gross tons (tonnes)

225,282 (228,897)	225,282 (228,897)	160,000 (162,567)	160,000 (162,567)	160,000 (162,567)
Oasis of the Seas	Allure of the Seas	Independence of the Seas	Liberty of the Seas	Freedom of the Seas

Fastest Plane

X-43A

NASA's experimental X-43A plane reached a top speed of Mach 9.8—or more than nine times the speed of sound—on a test flight over the Pacific Ocean in November 2004. The X-43A was mounted on top of a Pegasus rocket booster and was carried into the sky by a B-52 aircraft. The booster was then fired, taking the X-43A about 110,000 feet (33,530 m) above the ground. The rocket was detached from the unmanned X-43A, and the plane flew unassisted for several minutes. At this rate of 7,459 miles (12,004 km) per hour, a plane could circle Earth in just over three and a half hours!

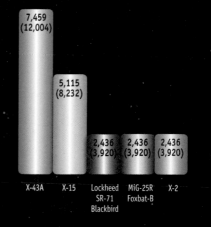

Fastest Planes

Maximum speed, in miles (kilometers) per hour

X-43A	X-15	Lockheed SR-71 Blackbird	MiG-25R Foxbat-B	X-2
7,459 (12,004)	5,115 (8,232)	2,436 (3,920)	2,436 (3,920)	2,436 (3,920)

Lightest Jet

BD-5J MICROJET

The BD-5J Microjet weighs only 358.8 pounds (162.7 kg), making it the lightest jet in the world. At only 12 feet (3.7 m) in length, it is one of the smallest as well. This tiny jet has a height of 5.6 feet (1.7 m) and a wingspan of 17 feet (5.2 m). The Microjet uses a TRS-18 turbojet engine. It can reach a top speed of 320 miles (514.9 km) per hour, but can only carry 32 gallons (121 L) of fuel at a time. A new BD-5J costs around $200,000. This high-tech gadget was flown by James Bond in the movie *Octopussy*, and it is also occasionally used by the US military.

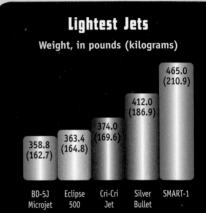

Lightest Jets

Weight, in pounds (kilograms)

BD-5J Microjet	Eclipse 500	Cri-Cri Jet	Silver Bullet	SMART-1
358.8 (162.7)	363.4 (164.8)	374.0 (169.6)	412.0 (186.9)	465.0 (210.9)

N3038V

Fastest Helicopter
V-22 OSPREY

The Bell Boeing V-22 Osprey can reach a top speed of 316 miles (509 kilometers) per hour. The Osprey has rotors that allow it to take off and land like a helicopter, but once it's airborne, its engine can rotate to turn the aircraft into a turboprop airplane. This makes the Osprey ideal for several different types of military missions, including combat support, long-range special ops, and search and rescue. The Osprey can carry 24 combat troops, as well as 20,000 pounds (9071 kg) of interior cargo or 15,000 pounds (6803 kg) of external cargo.

Fastest Helicopters

Maximum speed, in miles (kilometers) per hour

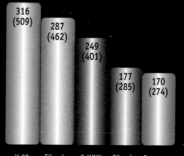

V-22 Osprey	Sikorsky X-2	G-LYNX	Sikorsky S76C	Eurocopter EC155 B1
316 (509)	287 (462)	249 (401)	177 (285)	170 (274)

Fastest Production Motorcycle

DUCATI DESMOSEDICI RR

The Ducati Desmosedici RR can speed down the street at 196 miles (315 km) per hour. That's about three times the speed limit on most US highways! This Italian street bike, which was originally created to race in the MotoGP World Championships, can accelerate from 0 to 60 miles (96 km) per hour in just 2.43 seconds. The liquid-cooled, 16-valve engine has four cylinders with gear-driven crankshafts. The Desmosedici uses Bridgestone tires and Brembo brakes. Only 1,500 of these special bikes were created, and the base price for each bike is $72,500.

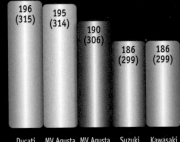

Fastest Production Motorcycles

Maximum speed, in miles (kilometers) per hour

Ducati Desmosedi-ci RR	MV Agusta F4 1100 CC	MV Agusta F4 1000 Tamburini	Suzuki GSX1300R Hayabusa	Kawasaki Ninja ZX-14
196 (315)	195 (314)	190 (306)	186 (299)	186 (299)

Tallest Roller Coaster
KINGDA KA

Kingda Ka towers over Six Flags Great Adventure in Jackson, New Jersey, at a height of 456 feet (139 m). Its highest drop plummets riders down 418 feet (127 m). The steel coaster can reach a top speed of 128 miles (206 km) per hour in just 3.5 seconds, and it was the fastest coaster in the world when it opened in 2005. The entire 3,118-foot (950 m) ride is over in just 28 seconds. The hydraulic launch coaster is located in the Golden Kingdom section of the park. It can accommodate about 1,400 riders per hour.

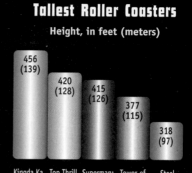

Tallest Roller Coasters
Height, in feet (meters)

Kingda Ka, USA	Top Thrill Dragster, USA	Superman: The Escape, USA	Tower of Terror, Australia	Steel Dragon 2000, Japan
456 (139)	420 (128)	415 (126)	377 (115)	318 (97)

Bestselling Cell Phone

APPLE 3G IPHONE

The Apple 3G iPhone was the bestselling cell phone in 2009, making up 4 percent of all mobile phone subscriptions. During 2009, customers bought about 25 million of these "smart phones." In addition to calling and texting, iPhone users can take videos, browse the Internet, and use their iTunes accounts. There are also tons of apps for the iPhone, ranging from recipes to games to health to business. The original iPhone was released in June 2007, and the 3G version came out in July 2008 with faster data speeds and GPS features.

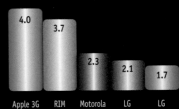

Bestselling Cell Phones

Percentage of total cell phone subscribers in 2009

Apple 3G iPhone	RIM Blackberry 8300 Series	Motorola RAZR V3 Series	LG VX9100	LG Voyager
4.0	3.7	2.3	2.1	1.7

Country with the Most Cell Phone Accounts

LITHUANIA

Lithuania has more than 138 cell phone accounts for every 100 people living there. That means there are about 5 million accounts in the small European country. Cell phones are quickly replacing many landlines throughout Lithuania. In fact, landline accounts dropped almost 40 percent while cell phone subscribers have risen 7 percent since 2007. This is because most cell phones now provide Internet access and computer features at a cheaper cost than traditional Internet service. The three main cell phone carriers in Lithuania are Omnitel, BITE, and TELE 2.

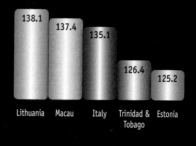

Countries with the Most Cell Phone Accounts

Cell phone accounts, per 100 people

Lithuania	Macau	Italy	Trinidad & Tobago	Estonia
138.1	137.4	135.1	126.4	125.2

Countries that Watch the Most TV

UNITED STATES & UNITED KINGDOM

Both the United Kingdom and the United States like to watch a lot of television, each averaging 38 hours of weekly program viewing per capita. That's the equivalent of almost 82 straight days, or 2.5 months per year! Some 98 percent of American households own at least one television, and about 54 percent of children have a set in their bedrooms. In the United Kingdom, about half the population watches free programming with basic channels, while the other half pays for cable and satellite TV. The most popular channels in the United Kingdom are BBC One, ITV, and Channel 4.

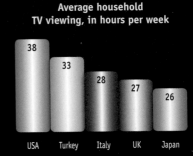

Countries that Watch the Most TV

Average household
TV viewing, in hours per week

USA	Turkey	Italy	UK	Japan
38	33	28	27	26

Country with the Most Television Sets
CHINA

China leads the world in television set ownership, with more than 380 million units. Approximately 80 percent of urban families and 30 percent of rural families have a set in their homes. There are more than 500 TV stations throughout the country. China Central Television, or CCTV as it's commonly known, is one of the largest networks in mainland China. CCTV's 19 channels reach about 1 billion viewers. About 55 percent of the population watches TV every day. Skyworth Digital Holdings is China's largest color television producer.

Countries with the Most Television Sets

Television sets, in millions

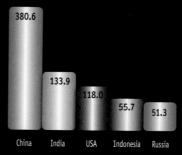

China	India	USA	Indonesia	Russia
380.6	133.9	118.0	55.7	51.3

143

NATURE RECORDS

Natural Formations Animals Weather
Plants Disasters Food Environment

Largest Diamond

GOLDEN JUBILEE

The Golden Jubilee is the world's largest faceted diamond, with a weight of 545.67 carats. This gigantic gem got its name when it was presented to the king of Thailand in 1997 for the Golden Jubilee—or 50th anniversary celebration—of his reign. The diamond weighed 755.5 carats when it was discovered in a South African mine in 1986. Once it was cut, the diamond featured 148 perfectly symmetrical facets. The process took almost a year because of the diamond's size and multiple tension points. The diamond is on display at the Royal Museum of Bangkok in Thailand.

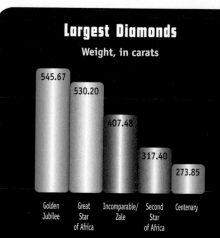

Largest Diamonds
Weight, in carats

Golden Jubilee	Great Star of Africa	Incomparable/ Zale	Second Star of Africa	Centenary
545.67	530.20	407.48	317.40	273.85

Tallest Mountain

MOUNT EVEREST

Mount Everest's tallest peak towers 29,035 feet (8,850 m) into the air, and it is the highest point on Earth. This peak is an unbelievable 5.5 miles (8.8 km) above sea level. Mount Everest is located in the Himalayas, on the border between Nepal and Tibet. The mountain got its official name from surveyor Sir George Everest. In 1953, Sir Edmund Hillary and Tenzing Norgay were the first people to reach the peak. In 2008, the Olympic torch was carried up to the top of the mountain on its way to the games in Beijing.

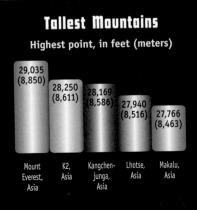

Tallest Mountains
Highest point, in feet (meters)

Mount Everest, Asia	K2, Asia	Kangchen- junga, Asia	Lhotse, Asia	Makalu, Asia
29,035 (8,850)	28,250 (8,611)	28,169 (8,586)	27,940 (8,516)	27,766 (8,463)

Tallest Volcano
OJOS DEL SALADO

Located on the border between Argentina and Chile, Ojos del Salado towers 22,595 feet (6,887 m) above the surrounding Atacama Desert. It is the second-highest peak in the Andean mountain chain. Ojos del Salado is a composite volcano, which means that it is a tall, symmetrical cone that was built by layers of lava flow, ash, and cinder. There is no record of the volcano erupting, but this could be because of the volcano's remote location. Ojos del Salado is a very popular spot for mountain climbing.

Tallest Volcanoes
Height, in feet (meters)

Ojos del Salado, Argentina/Chile	Llullaillaco, Argentina/Chile	Tipas, Argentina	Nevado de Incahussi, Argentina/Chile	Cerro el Cóndor, Argentina
22,595 (6,887)	22,109 (6,739)	21,850 (6,660)	21,722 (6,621)	21,430 (6,532)

Largest Lake

CASPIAN SEA

This giant inland body of salt water stretches for almost 750 miles (1,207 km) from north to south, with an average width of about 200 miles (322 km). Altogether, it covers an area that's almost the same size as the state of California. The Caspian Sea is located east of the Caucasus Mountains in central Asia. It is bordered by Iran, Russia, Kazakhstan, Azerbaijan, and Turkmenistan. The Caspian Sea has an average depth of about 550 feet (170 m). It is an important fishing resource, with species including sturgeon, salmon, perch, herring, and carp. Other animals living in the Caspian Sea include porpoises, seals, and tortoises. The sea is estimated to be 30 million years old and became landlocked 5.5 million years ago.

Largest Lakes

Approximate area, in
square miles (square kilometers)

Caspian Sea, Asia	Superior, N. America	Victoria, Africa	Huron, N. America	Michigan, N. America
143,200 (370,901)	31,820 (82,413)	26,828 (69,485)	23,010 (59,596)	22,400 (58,016)

Largest Desert

SAHARA

Located in northern Africa, the Sahara Desert covers approximately 3.5 million square miles (9.1 million sq km). It stretches for 5,200 miles (8,372 km) through the countries of Morocco, Algeria, Tunisia, Libya, Egypt, Mauritania, Mali, Niger, Chad, and Sudan. The Sahara gets very little rainfall—less than 8 inches (20 cm) per year. Even with its harsh environment, some 2.5 million people—mostly nomads—call the Sahara home. Date palms and acacias grow near oases. Some of the animals that live in the Sahara include gazelles, antelopes, jackals, foxes, and badgers.

Largest Deserts

Area, in millions of square miles (square kilometers)

Sahara, Africa	Arabian, Asia	Gobi, Asia	Kalahari, Africa	Patagonia, South America
3.50 (9.10)	0.90 (2.30)	0.50 (1.30)	0.36 (0.90)	0.26 (0.67)

Longest River

NILE

The Nile River in Africa stretches 4,145 miles (6,671 km) from the tributaries of Lake Victoria in Tanzania and Uganda out to the Mediterranean Sea. Because of varying depths, boats can sail on only about 2,000 miles (3,217 km) of the river. The Nile flows through Rwanda, Uganda, Sudan, and Egypt. The river's water supply is crucial to the existence of these African countries. The Nile's precious water is used to irrigate crops and to generate electricity. The Aswan Dam and the Aswan High Dam—both located in Egypt—are used to store the autumn floodwater for later use. The Nile is also used to transport goods from city to city along the river.

Longest Rivers

Total length, in miles (kilometers)

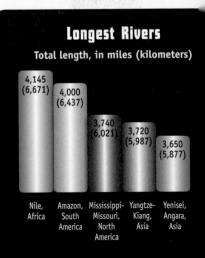

Nile, Africa	Amazon, South America	Mississippi- Missouri, North America	Yangtze- Kiang, Asia	Yenisei, Angara, Asia
4,145 (6,671)	4,000 (6,437)	3,740 (6,021)	3,720 (5,987)	3,650 (5,877)

Largest Ocean
PACIFIC

The Pacific Ocean covers almost 64 million square miles (166 million sq km) and reaches 36,200 feet (11,000 m) below sea level at its greatest depth—the Mariana Trench (near the Philippines). In fact, this ocean is so large that it covers about one-third of the planet (more than all of Earth's land put together) and holds more than half of all the seawater on Earth. The United States could fit inside this ocean 18 times! Some of the major bodies of water included in the Pacific are the Bering Sea, the Coral Sea, the Philippine Sea, and the Gulf of Alaska.

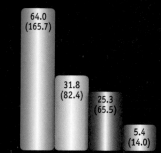

Largest Oceans

Approximate area, in millions of square miles (square kilometers)

Pacific Ocean	Atlantic Ocean	Indian Ocean	Arctic Ocean
64.0 (165.7)	31.8 (82.4)	25.3 (65.5)	5.4 (14.0)

Largest Island
GREENLAND

Located in the North Atlantic Ocean, Greenland covers more than 840,000 square miles (2,175,600 sq km). Not including continents, it is the largest island in the world. Its jagged coastline is approximately 24,400 miles (39,267 km) long—about the same distance as Earth's circumference at the equator. Mountain chains are located on Greenland's east and west coasts, and the coastline is indented by fjords, or thin bodies of water bordered by steep cliffs. From north to south, the island stretches for about 1,660 miles (2,670 km). About 700,000 square miles (1,813,000 sq km) of this massive island are covered by a giant ice sheet. The island also contains the world's largest national park—Northeast Greenland National Park—with an area of 375,291 square miles (972,000 sq km).

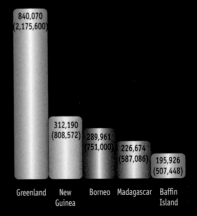

Largest Islands

Approximate area, in square miles (square kilometers)

Greenland	New Guinea	Borneo	Madagascar	Baffin Island
840,070 (2,175,600)	312,190 (808,572)	289,961 (751,000)	226,674 (587,086)	195,926 (507,448)

Country with the Most Tropical Rain Forests

BRAZIL

Brazil—a large, tropical country in South America—has almost 1.15 million square miles (3.0 million sq km) of rain forest. The tropical forests of the Amazon River are located in the northern and north central areas of the country. Amazonia, the world's largest rain forest, spreads across half of Brazil. The rain forest is home to 2.5 million species of insect, 500 mammal species, 300 reptile species, and a third of the world's birds. The rain forest is threatened, however, by timber companies, the growing human population, and ranchers clearing land for their herds to graze.

Countries with the Most Tropical Rain Forests

Area of rain forest, in square miles (square kilometers)

Brazil, South America	Democratic Republic of Congo, Africa	Indonesia, Asia	Peru, South America	Bolivia, South America
1,157,295 (2,997,380)	515,871 (1,336,099)	341,681 (884,949)	235,773 (610,649)	226,796 (587,398)

Largest Crustacean
GIANT SPIDER CRAB

The giant spider crab has a 12-foot (3.7 m) leg span. That's almost wide enough to take up two parking spaces! The crab's body measures about 15 inches (38.1 cm) wide. Its ten long legs are jointed, and the first set has large claws at the end. The giant sea creature can weigh between 35 and 44 pounds (16 and 20 kg). It feeds on dead animals and shellfish it finds on the ocean floor. Giant spider crabs live in the deep water of the Pacific Ocean off southern Japan.

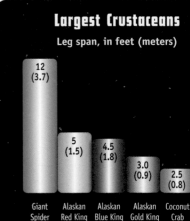

Largest Crustaceans
Leg span, in feet (meters)

Giant Spider Crab	Alaskan Red King Crab	Alaskan Blue King Crab	Alaskan Gold King Crab	Coconut Crab
12 (3.7)	5 (1.5)	4.5 (1.8)	3.0 (0.9)	2.5 (0.8)

Loudest Animal

BLUE WHALE

The loudest animal on Earth is the blue whale. The giant mammal's call can reach up to 188 decibels—about 40 decibels louder than a jet engine. The rumbling, low-frequency sounds of the blue whale can be heard for several hundred miles below the sea. Much of this whale chatter is used for communication, especially during the mating season. People cannot detect the whales' calls because they are too low-pitched for human ears.

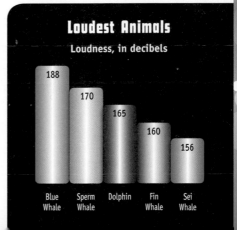

Loudest Animals

Loudness, in decibels

Blue Whale	Sperm Whale	Dolphin	Fin Whale	Sei Whale
188	170	165	160	156

Biggest Fish

WHALE SHARK

Although the average length of a whale shark is 30 feet (9 m), many have been known to reach up to 60 feet (18 m) long. That's the same length as two school buses! Whale sharks also weigh an average of 50,000 pounds (22,680 kg). As with most sharks, the females are larger than the males. Their mouths measure about 5 feet (1.5 m) long and contain about 3,000 teeth. Amazingly, these gigantic fish eat only microscopic plankton and tiny fish. They float near the surface looking for food.

Biggest Fish

Average weight, in pounds (kilograms)

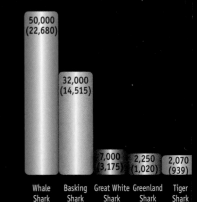

Whale Shark	Basking Shark	Great White Shark	Greenland Shark	Tiger Shark
50,000 (22,680)	32,000 (14,515)	7,000 (3,175)	2,250 (1,020)	2,070 (939)

Most Dangerous Shark
GREAT WHITE

With a total of 244 unprovoked attacks on humans, great white sharks are the most dangerous predators in the sea. A great white can measure more than 20 feet (6.1 m) in length and weigh up to 3,800 pounds (1,723 kg). Because of the sharks' size, they can feed on large prey, including seals, dolphins, and even small whales. Often, when a human is attacked by a great white, it is because the shark has mistaken the person for its typical prey. The sharks make their homes in most waters throughout the world, but are most frequently found off the coasts of Australia, South Africa, California, and Mexico.

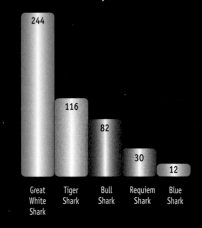

Most Dangerous Sharks
Number of unprovoked attacks

Great White Shark	Tiger Shark	Bull Shark	Requiem Shark	Blue Shark
244	116	82	30	12

Whale that Dives the Deepest

SPERM WHALE

Sperm whales can dive down to 10,500 feet (3,200 m) below the sea. The whales dive so deeply to hunt for giant squid to feed on. These dives last about 40 minutes, but a sperm whale can hold its breath for about an hour. The whales spend about 10 minutes at the surface of the water between deep dives. The sperm whale also holds the record for the largest animal brain, weighing in at about 20 pounds (9.1 kg). The whales can grow up to 60 feet (18.2 m) in length, and weigh up to 50 tons (45.4 t).

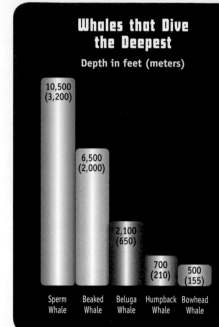

Whales that Dive the Deepest

Depth in feet (meters)

Sperm Whale	Beaked Whale	Beluga Whale	Humpback Whale	Bowhead Whale
10,500 (3,200)	6,500 (2,000)	2,100 (650)	700 (210)	500 (155)

Fastest Fish

SAILFISH

A sailfish once grabbed a fishing line and dragged it 300 feet (91 m) away in just three seconds. That means it was swimming at an average speed of 69 miles (109 km) per hour—higher than the average speed limit on a highway! Sailfish are very large—they average 6 feet (1.8 m) long, but can grow up to 11 feet (3.4 m). Sailfish eat squid and surface-dwelling fish. Sometimes several sailfish will work together to catch their prey. They are found in both the Atlantic and Pacific oceans and prefer a water temperature of about 80°F (27°C).

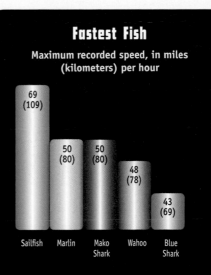

Fastest Fish

Maximum recorded speed, in miles (kilometers) per hour

Sailfish	Marlin	Mako Shark	Wahoo	Blue Shark
69 (109)	50 (80)	50 (80)	48 (78)	43 (69)

159

Fastest Shark

MAKO SHARK

A mako shark can cruise through the water at 50 miles (79.4 km) per hour. This super speed helps the shark catch its food, which consists mostly of tuna, herring, mackerel, swordfish, and porpoise. Occasionally makos even build up enough speed to leap out of the water. Mako sharks average 7 feet (2.1 m) in length, but can grow up to 12 feet (3.7 m) and weigh on average 1,000 pounds (454 kg). The sharks are found in temperate and tropical seas throughout the world.

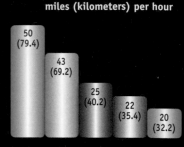

Fastest Sharks

Fastest speed, in
miles (kilometers) per hour

Mako Shark	Blue Shark	Great White Shark	Tiger Shark	Lemon Shark
50 (79.4)	43 (69.2)	25 (40.2)	22 (35.4)	20 (32.2)

Heaviest Marine Mammal

BLUE WHALE

Blue whales are the largest animals that have ever inhabited Earth. They can weigh more than 143.3 tons (130 t) and measure over 100 feet (30 m) long. Amazingly, these gentle giants only eat krill—small, shrimplike animals. A blue whale can eat about 4 tons (3.6 t) of krill each day in the summer, when food is plentiful. To catch the krill, a whale gulps as much as 17,000 gallons (64,600 L) of seawater into its mouth at one time. Then it uses its tongue—which can be as big as a car—to push the water back out. The krill get caught in hairs on the whale's baleen (a keratin structure that hangs down from the roof of the whale's mouth).

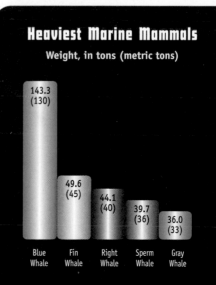

Heaviest Marine Mammals

Weight, in tons (metric tons)

Blue Whale	Fin Whale	Right Whale	Sperm Whale	Gray Whale
143.3 (130)	49.6 (45)	44.1 (40)	39.7 (36)	36.0 (33)

Largest Bird Wingspan
MARABOU STORK

With a wingspan that can reach up to 13 feet (4 m), the marabou stork has the largest wingspan of any bird. These large storks weigh up to 20 pounds (9 kg) and can grow up to 5 feet (150 cm) tall. Their long leg and toe bones are actually hollow. This adaptation is very important for flight because it makes the bird lighter. Although marabous eat insects, small mammals, and fish, the majority of their food is carrion—meat that is already dead. In fact, the stork's head and neck do not have any feathers. This helps the bird stay clean as it sticks its head into carcasses to pick out scraps of food.

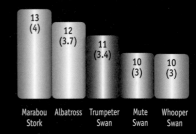

Largest Bird Wingspans
Wingspan, in feet (meters)

Marabou Stork	Albatross	Trumpeter Swan	Mute Swan	Whooper Swan
13 (4)	12 (3.7)	11 (3.4)	10 (3)	10 (3)

Fastest Flier

PEREGRINE FALCON

A peregrine falcon can reach speeds of up to 175 miles (282 km) per hour while diving through the air. That's about the same speed as the fastest race car in the Indianapolis 500. These powerful birds can catch prey in midair and kill it instantly with their sharp claws. Peregrine falcons range from about 13 to 19 inches (33 to 48 cm) long. The female is called a falcon, but the male is called a tercel, which means "one-third" in German. This is because the male is about one-third the size of the female.

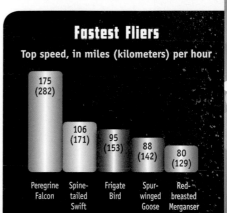

Fastest Fliers

Top speed, in miles (kilometers) per hour

Peregrine Falcon	Spine-tailed Swift	Frigate Bird	Spur-winged Goose	Red-breasted Merganser
175 (282)	106 (171)	95 (153)	88 (142)	80 (129)

Longest Bird Migration
ARCTIC TERN

The arctic tern migrates from Maine to the coast of Africa, and then on to Antarctica, flying some 22,000 miles (35,406 km) a year. That's almost the same distance as the Earth's circumference. Some don't complete the journey, however—young terns fly the first half of the journey with their parents, but remain in Antarctica for a year or two. When they have matured, the birds fly back to Maine and the surrounding areas. Scientists are puzzled about how these birds remember the way back after only making the journey once, so early in their lives.

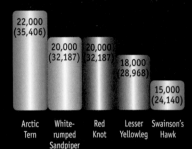

Longest Bird Migrations
Round-trip migration, in miles (kilometers)

Arctic Tern	White-rumped Sandpiper	Red Knot	Lesser Yellowleg	Swainson's Hawk
22,000 (35,406)	20,000 (32,187)	20,000 (32,187)	18,000 (28,968)	15,000 (24,140)

Bird that Builds the Largest Nest

BALD EAGLE

With a nest that can measure 8 feet (2.4 m) wide and 16 feet (4.9 m) deep, bald eagles have plenty of room to move around. These birds of prey have wingspans of up to 7.5 feet (2.3 m) and need a home that they can nest in comfortably. By carefully constructing their nest with sticks, branches, and plant material, a pair of bald eagles can balance their home—which can weigh up to 4,000 pounds (1,814 kg)—on the top of a tree or cliff. These nests are usually located by rivers or coastlines, the birds' watery hunting grounds. Called an aerie, this home will be used for the rest of the eagles' lives.

Birds that Build the Largest Nests

Nest diameter, in feet (meters)

Bald Eagle	Sociable Weaver	Maguari Stork	Great Blue Heron	Monk Parakeet
8 (2.4)	7 (2.1)	6 (1.8)	4.5 (1.4)	3 (0.9)

Largest Bird Egg

OSTRICH EGG

Ostriches—the world's largest birds—can lay eggs that measure 5 inches by 6 inches (13 cm by 16 cm) and weigh up to 4 pounds (1.8 kg). In fact, just one ostrich egg weighs as much as 24 chicken eggs. The egg yolk makes up one-third of the volume. Although the eggshell is only 0.08 inches (2 mm) thick, it is tough enough to withstand the weight of a 345-pound (157 kg) ostrich. A hen ostrich can lay from 10 to 70 eggs each year. Females are usually able to recognize their own eggs, even when they are mixed in with those of other females in their shared nest.

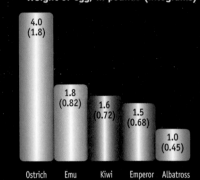

Largest Bird Eggs

Weight of egg, in pounds (kilograms)

Ostrich	Emu	Kiwi	Emperor Penguin	Albatross
4.0 (1.8)	1.8 (0.82)	1.6 (0.72)	1.5 (0.68)	1.0 (0.45)

Fastest Land Bird

OSTRICH

An ostrich can run at a top speed of 45 miles (72.4 km) per hour for about 30 minutes. This allows the speedy bird to easily outrun most predators. Its long, powerful legs help an ostrich cover 10 to 15 feet (3.1 to 4.6 km) per bound. And although it is a flightless bird, an ostrich uses its wings for balance when it runs. If an ostrich does need to defend itself, it has a kick powerful enough to kill a lion. The ostrich, which is also the world's largest bird at 10 feet (3.1 m) tall and 350 pounds (158.8 kg), is native to the savannas of Africa.

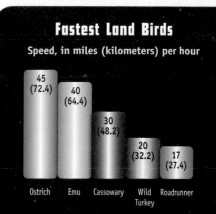

Fastest Land Birds

Speed, in miles (kilometers) per hour

Ostrich	Emu	Cassowary	Wild Turkey	Roadrunner
45 (72.4)	40 (64.4)	30 (48.2)	20 (32.2)	17 (27.4)

Heaviest Land Mammal

AFRICAN ELEPHANT

Weighing in at up to 14,430 pounds (6,545 kg) and measuring approximately 24 feet (7.3 m) long, African elephants are truly humongous. Even at their great size, they are strictly vegetarian. They will, however, eat up to 500 pounds (226 kg) of vegetation a day! Their two tusks—which are actually elongated teeth—grow continuously during their lives and can reach about 9 feet (2.7 m) in length. Elephants live in small groups of 8 to 15 family members with one female (called a cow) as the leader.

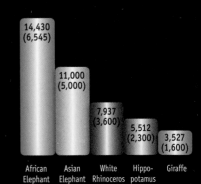

Heaviest Land Mammals
Weight, in pounds (kilograms)

14,430 (6,545)	11,000 (5,000)	7,937 (3,600)	5,512 (2,300)	3,527 (1,600)
African Elephant	Asian Elephant	White Rhinoceros	Hippo-potamus	Giraffe

Largest Rodent

CAPYBARA

Capybaras reach an average length of 4 feet (1.2 m), stand about 20 inches (51 cm) tall, and weigh between 75 and 150 pounds (34 to 68 kg)! That's about the same size as a Labrador retriever. Also known as water hogs and carpinchos, capybaras are found in South and Central America, where they spend much of their time in groups, looking for food. They are strictly vegetarian and have been known to raid gardens for melons and squash. Their partially webbed feet make capybaras excellent swimmers. They can dive down to the bottom of a lake or river to find plants and stay there for up to five minutes.

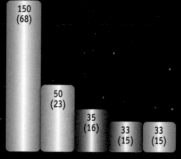

Largest Rodents
Weight, in pounds (kilograms)

Capybara	Beaver	Porcupine	Pacarana	Patagonian Cavy
150 (68)	50 (23)	35 (16)	33 (15)	33 (15)

Slowest Land Mammal

THREE-TOED SLOTH

A three-toed sloth can reach a top speed of only 0.07 miles (0.11 km) per hour while traveling on the ground. That means that it would take the animal almost 15 minutes to cross a four-lane street. The main reason sloths move so slowly is that they cannot walk like other mammals. They must pull themselves along the ground using only their sharp claws. Because of this, sloths spend the majority of their time in trees. There, they will sleep up to 18 hours each day. When they wake at night, they search for leaves and shoots to eat.

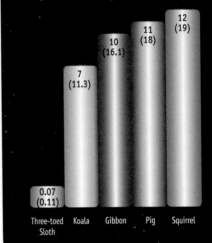

Some of the Slowest Land Mammals
Speed, in miles (kilometers) per hour

Three-toed Sloth	Koala	Gibbon	Pig	Squirrel
0.07 (0.11)	7 (11.3)	10 (16.1)	11 (18)	12 (19)

Fastest Land Mammal

CHEETAH

For short spurts, these sleek mammals can reach a speed of 65 miles (105 km) per hour. They can accelerate from 0 to 40 miles (64 km) per hour in just three strides. Their quickness easily enables these large African cats to outrun their prey. All other African cats must stalk their prey because they lack the cheetah's amazing speed. Unlike the paws of all other cats, cheetah paws do not have skin sheaths (thin protective coverings). Their claws, therefore, cannot be retracted.

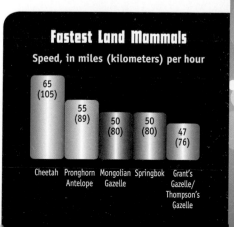

Fastest Land Mammals

Speed, in miles (kilometers) per hour

Cheetah	Pronghorn Antelope	Mongolian Gazelle	Springbok	Grant's Gazelle/ Thompson's Gazelle
65 (105)	55 (89)	50 (80)	50 (80)	47 (76)

Tallest Land Animal

GIRAFFE

Giraffes are the giants among mammals, growing to more than 18 feet (5.5 m) in height. That means an average giraffe could look through the window of a two-story building. A giraffe's neck is 18 times longer than a human's, but both mammals have exactly the same number of neck bones. A giraffe's long legs enable it to outrun most of its enemies. When cornered, a giraffe has been known to kill a lion with a single kick to the head.

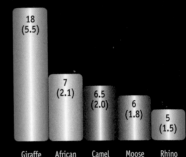

Some of the Tallest Land Animals

Height, in feet (meters)

Giraffe	African Elephant	Camel	Moose	Rhino
18 (5.5)	7 (2.1)	6.5 (2.0)	6 (1.8)	5 (1.5)

Largest Bat

GIANT FLYING FOX

The giant flying fox—a member of the megabat family—can have a wingspan of up to 6 feet (2 m). These furry mammals average just 7 wing beats per second, but can travel more than 40 miles (64 km) a night in search of food. Unlike smaller bats, which use echolocation, flying foxes rely on their acute vision and sense of smell to locate fruit, pollen, and nectar. Flying foxes got their name because their faces resemble a fox's face. Megabats live in the tropical areas of Africa, Asia, and Australia.

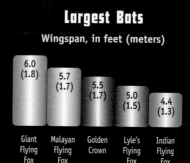

Largest Bats

Wingspan, in feet (meters)

Giant Flying Fox	Malayan Flying Fox	Golden Crown	Lyle's Flying Fox	Indian Flying Fox
6.0 (1.8)	5.7 (1.7)	5.5 (1.7)	5.0 (1.5)	4.4 (1.3)

Deadliest Amphibian

POISON DART FROG

Poison dart frogs are found mostly in the tropical rain forests of Central and South America, where they live on the moist land. These lethal amphibians have enough poison to kill up to 20 humans. A dart frog's poison is so effective that native Central and South Americans sometimes coat their hunting arrows or hunting darts with it. These brightly colored frogs can be yellow, orange, red, green, blue, or any combination of these colors. They measure only 0.5 to 2 inches (1 to 5 cm) long. There are approximately 75 different species of poison dart frogs.

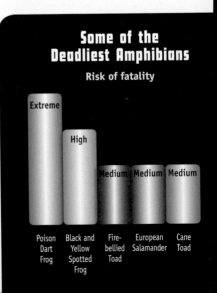

Some of the Deadliest Amphibians

Risk of fatality

Extreme	High	Medium	Medium	Medium
Poison Dart Frog	Black and Yellow Spotted Frog	Fire-bellied Toad	European Salamander	Cane Toad

Longest Snake
RETICULATED PYTHON

Some adult reticulated pythons can grow to 27 feet (8.2 m) long, but most reach an average length of 17 feet (5 m). That's almost the length of an average school bus! These pythons live mostly in Asia, from Myanmar to Indonesia to the Philippines. The python has teeth that curve backward to hold its prey still. It hunts mainly at night and will eat mammals and birds. Reticulated pythons are slow-moving creatures that kill their prey by constriction, or strangulation.

Longest Snakes
Maximum length, in feet (meters)

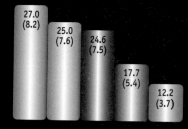

Reticulated Python	Anaconda	Rock Python	King Cobra	Oriental Rat Snake
27.0 (8.2)	25.0 (7.6)	24.6 (7.5)	17.7 (5.4)	12.2 (3.7)

Snake with the Longest Fangs
GABOON VIPER

The fangs of a Gaboon viper measure 2 inches (5.1 cm) in length! These giant fangs fold up against the snake's mouth so it does not pierce its own skin. When it is ready to strike its prey, the fangs snap down into position. The snake can grow up to 7 feet (2 m) long and weigh 18 pounds (8 kg). It is found in Africa and is perfectly camouflaged for hunting on the ground beneath leaves and grasses. The Gaboon viper's poison is not as toxic as some other snakes', but it is quite dangerous because of the amount of poison it can inject at one time. The snake is not very aggressive, however, and usually only attacks when bothered.

Snakes with the Longest Fangs

Fang length, in inches (centimeters)

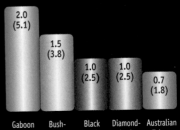

Gaboon Viper	Bush-master	Black Mamba	Diamond-back Rattlesnake	Australian Taipan
2.0 (5.1)	1.5 (3.8)	1.0 (2.5)	1.0 (2.5)	0.7 (1.8)

Deadliest Snake
BLACK MAMBA

With just one bite, an African black mamba snake releases a venom powerful enough to kill up to 200 humans. A bite from this snake is almost always fatal if it is not treated immediately. This large member of the cobra family grows to about 14 feet (4.3 m) long. In addition to its deadly poison, it is a very aggressive snake. It will raise its body off the ground when it feels threatened. It then spreads its hood and strikes swiftly at its prey with its long front teeth. A black mamba is also very fast—it can move along at about 7 miles (11.7 km) per hour for short bursts.

Deadliest Snakes
Human deaths possible per bite

Black Mamba	Taipan	Russell's Viper	Common Krait	Forest Cobra
200	170	150	60	50

Largest Amphibian

CHINESE GIANT SALAMANDER

With a length of 6 feet (1.8 m) and a weight of 55 pounds (25 kg), Chinese giant salamanders rule the amphibian world. This salamander has a large head, but its eyes and nostrils are small. It has short legs, a long tail, and very smooth skin. This large creature can be found in the streams of northeastern, central, and southern China. It feeds on fish, frogs, crabs, and snakes. The Chinese giant salamander will not hunt its prey. It will wait until a potential meal wanders too close and then grab it in its mouth. Because many people enjoy the taste of the salamander's meat, it is often hunted and its population is shrinking.

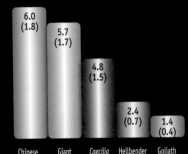

Largest Amphibians

Maximum length, in feet (meters)

Chinese Giant Salamander	Giant Japanese Salamander	*Caecilia Thompsoni*	Hellbender	Goliath Frog
6.0 (1.8)	5.7 (1.7)	4.8 (1.5)	2.4 (0.7)	1.4 (0.4)

Longest-Lived Reptile

GALÁPAGOS TORTOISE

Some Galápagos tortoises have been known to live to the old age of 150 years. Galápagos tortoises are also some of the largest tortoises in the world, weighing in at up to 500 pounds (226 kg). These creatures are able to pull their heads, tails, and legs completely inside their shells. Amazingly, Galápagos tortoises can go without eating or drinking for many weeks. Approximately 10,000 of these tortoises live on the Galápagos island chain west of Ecuador.

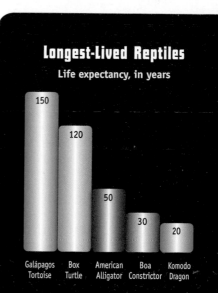

Longest-Lived Reptiles

Life expectancy, in years

Galápagos Tortoise	Box Turtle	American Alligator	Boa Constrictor	Komodo Dragon
150	120	50	30	20

Largest Lizard

KOMODO DRAGON

With a length of 10 feet (3 m) and a weight of 300 pounds (136 kg), Komodo dragons are the largest lizards roaming the earth. A Komodo dragon has a long neck and tail, and strong legs. These members of the monitor family are found mainly on Komodo Island, located in the Lesser Sunda Islands of Indonesia. Komodos are dangerous and have even been known to attack and kill humans. A Komodo uses its sense of smell to locate food, using its long, yellow tongue. A Komodo can consume 80 percent of its body weight in just one meal!

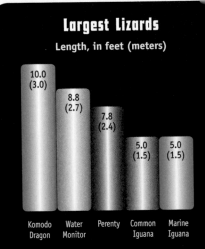

Largest Lizards

Length, in feet (meters)

Komodo Dragon	Water Monitor	Perenty	Common Iguana	Marine Iguana
10.0 (3.0)	8.8 (2.7)	7.8 (2.4)	5.0 (1.5)	5.0 (1.5)

Largest Reptile
SALTWATER CROCODILE

Saltwater crocodiles can grow to 22 feet (6.7 m) long. That's about twice the length of the average car. However, males usually measure only about 17 feet (5 m) long, and females normally reach about 10 feet (3 m) in length. A large adult will feed on buffalo, monkeys, cattle, wild boar, and other large mammals. Saltwater crocodiles are found throughout the East Indies and Australia. Despite their name, saltwater crocodiles can also be found in fresh water and swamps. Some other common names for this species are the estuary crocodile and the Indo-Pacific crocodile.

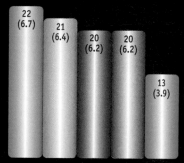

Largest Reptiles
Maximum length, in feet (meters)

22 (6.7)	21 (6.4)	20 (6.2)	20 (6.2)	13 (3.9)
Saltwater Crocodile	Gharial	Black Caiman	Orinoco Crocodile	American Alligator

Largest Spider

GOLIATH BIRDEATER

A Goliath birdeater is about the same size as a dinner plate—it can grow to a total length of 11 inches (28 cm) and weigh about 6 ounces (170 g). A Goliath's spiderlings are also big—they can have a 6-inch (15 cm) leg span just one year after hatching. These giant tarantulas are found mostly in the rain forests of Guyana, Suriname, Brazil, and Venezuela. The Goliath birdeater's name is misleading—they commonly eat insects and small reptiles. Similar to other tarantula species, the Goliath birdeater lives in a burrow. The spider will wait by the opening to ambush prey that gets too close.

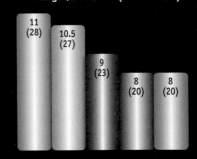

Largest Spiders
Length, in inches (centimeters)

Goliath Birdeater	Salmon Pink Birdeater	Slate Red Ornamental	King Baboon	Colombian Giant Redleg
11 (28)	10.5 (27)	9 (23)	8 (20)	8 (20)

Fastest-Flying Insect

HAWK MOTH

The average hawk moth—which got its name from its swift and steady flight—can cruise along at speeds over 33 miles (53 km) per hour. That's faster than the average speed limit on most city streets. Although they are found throughout the world, most live in tropical climates. Also known as the sphinx moth and the hummingbird moth, this large insect can have a wingspan that reaches up to 8 inches (20 cm). The insect also has a good memory and may return to the same flowers at the same time each day.

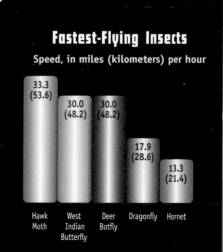

Fastest-Flying Insects

Speed, in miles (kilometers) per hour

Insect	Speed
Hawk Moth	33.3 (53.6)
West Indian Butterfly	30.0 (48.2)
Deer Botfly	30.0 (48.2)
Dragonfly	17.9 (28.6)
Hornet	13.3 (21.4)

Fastest-Running Insect
AUSTRALIAN TIGER BEETLE

Australian tiger beetles can zip along at about 5.7 miles (9.2 km) per hour—that's about 170 body lengths per second! If a human could run at the same pace, he or she would run about 340 miles (547.2 km) per hour. Australian tiger beetles use their terrific speed to run down prey. Once a meal has been caught, the beetle chews it up in its powerful jaws and coats it in digestive juice. When the prey has become soft, the tiger beetle rolls it together and eats it. These fierce beetles, which got their name from their skillful hunting, will also bite humans when provoked.

Fastest-Running Insects
Speed, in miles (kilometers) per hour

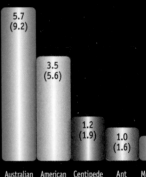

Australian Tiger Beetle	American Cockroach	Centipede	Ant	Mother-of-Pearl Caterpillar
5.7 (9.2)	3.5 (5.6)	1.2 (1.9)	1.0 (1.6)	0.8 (1.3)

Longest Insect Migration

MONARCH BUTTERFLY

Millions of monarch butterflies travel to Mexico from all parts of North America every fall, flying as far as 2,700 miles (4,345 km). Once there, they will huddle together in the trees and wait out the cold weather. In spring and summer, most butterflies only live four or five weeks as adults, but in the fall, a special generation of monarchs is born. These butterflies will live for about seven months and participate in the great migration to Mexico. Scientists are studying these butterflies in the hope of learning how the insects know where and when to migrate to a place they have never visited before.

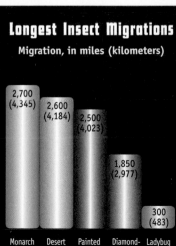

Longest Insect Migrations

Migration, in miles (kilometers)

Monarch Butterfly	Desert Locust	Painted Lady Butterfly	Diamond-back Moth	Ladybug
2,700 (4,345)	2,600 (4,184)	2,500 (4,023)	1,850 (2,977)	300 (483)

Most Common Pet in the United States

DOGS

There are 45.6 million households across the United States that own one or more dogs. That means that about 39 percent of homes in America have a pooch residing there. About 24 percent of these families own two dogs, while another 9 percent own three or more. When it comes to finding a dog, approximately 19 percent of families head to a shelter to adopt one. Those who prefer purebreds tend to choose Labrador retrievers, German shepherds, and Yorkshire terriers. Some of the most popular dog names include Max, Buddy, Rocky, and Bailey.

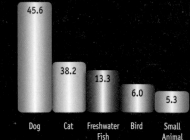

Most Common Pets in the United States

US households that own a pet, in millions

Dog	Cat	Freshwater Fish	Bird	Small Animal
45.6	38.2	13.3	6.0	5.3

Highest US Pet Population

FRESHWATER FISH

There are more than 171.7 million freshwater fish living in homes across the United States. Some 13.3 million households in the country own these finned creatures. Fish are very popular pets because they take up less space and require less attention than most other animals. Some of the most popular freshwater fish include goldfish, guppies, betas, and mollies. Pets play an important role in the United States, residing in more than 62 percent of all homes. Pet owners shell out about $47.7 million each year to care for their animal friends.

Highest US Pet Populations

Number of pets, in millions

Freshwater Fish	Cats	Dogs	Small Animals	Birds
171.7	93.6	77.5	15.9	15.0

United States' Greatest Annual Snowfall

MOUNT RAINIER

Mount Rainier had a record snowfall of 1,224 inches (3,109 cm) between February 1971 and February 1972. That's enough snow to cover a ten-story building! Located in the Cascade Mountains of Washington State, Mount Rainier is actually a volcano buried under 35 square miles (90.7 sq km) of snow and ice. The mountain, which covers about 100 square miles (259 sq km), reaches a height of 14,410 feet (4,392 m). Its three peaks include Liberty Cap, Point Success, and Columbia Crest. Mt. Rainier National Park was established in 1899.

United States' Greatest Annual Snowfalls

Highest annual snowfall, in inches (centimeters)

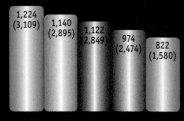

Mount Rainier, Washington, Feb. 1971–Feb. 1972	Mount Baker, Washington, 1998–1999	Paradise Station, Washington, July 1, 1971–June 30, 1972	Thompson Pass, Alaska, 1952–1953	Crater Lake National Park, Oregon 1948–1949
1,224 (3,109)	1,140 (2,895)	1,122 (2,849)	974 (2,474)	822 (1,580)

Coldest Inhabited Place

RESOLUTE

The residents of Resolute, Canada, have to bundle up—the average annual temperature is just -11.6°F (-24.2°C). Located on the northeast shore of Resolute Bay on the south coast of Cornwallis Island, the community is commonly the starting point for expeditions to the North Pole. In the winter it can stay dark for 24 hours, and in the summer it can stay light during the entire night. Only about 200 people brave the climate year-round, but the area is becoming quite popular with tourists.

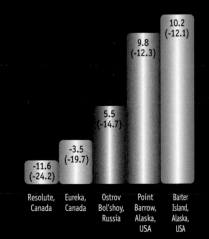

Coldest Inhabited Places

Average annual temperature, in degrees Fahrenheit (Celsius)

Resolute, Canada	Eureka, Canada	Ostrov Bol'shoy, Russia	Point Barrow, Alaska, USA	Barter Island, Alaska, USA
-11.6 (-24.2)	-3.5 (-19.7)	5.5 (-14.7)	9.8 (-12.3)	10.2 (-12.1)

Hottest
Inhabited Place

DALLOL

Throughout the year, temperatures in Dallol, Ethiopia, average 93.2°F (34.0°C). Dallol is at the northernmost tip of the Great Rift Valley. The Dallol Depression reaches 328 feet (100 m) below sea level, making it the lowest point below sea level that is not covered by water. The area also has several active volcanoes. The only people to inhabit the region are the Afar, who have adapted to the harsh conditions there. For instance, to collect water the women build covered stone piles and wait for condensation to form on the rocks.

Hottest Inhabited Places

Average temperature, in degrees Fahrenheit (Celsius)

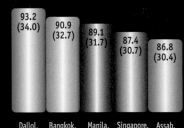

Dallol, Ethiopia	Bangkok, Thailand	Manila, Philippines	Singapore, Singapore	Assab, Eritrea
93.2 (34.0)	90.9 (32.7)	89.1 (31.7)	87.4 (30.7)	86.8 (30.4)

Wettest Inhabited Place

LLORO

Umbrellas are in constant use in Lloro, Colombia, where the average annual rainfall totals about 523 inches (1,328 cm). That's about 1.4 inches (3.5 cm) a day, totaling more than 43 feet (13 m) a year! Located in the northwestern part of the country, Lloro is near the Pacific Ocean and the Caribbean Sea. Trade winds help bring lots of moisture from the coasts to this tropical little town, creating the humidity and precipitation that soak this lowland. Lloro is home to about 7,000 people.

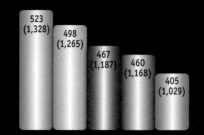

Wettest Inhabited Places

Average annual rainfall, in inches (centimeters)

Lloro, Colombia	Cherrapunji, India	Mawsynram, India	Waialeale, Hawaii, USA	Debundscha, Cameroon
523 (1,328)	498 (1,265)	467 (1,187)	460 (1,168)	405 (1,029)

Driest Inhabited Place

ASWAN

Each year, only 0.02 inches (0.5 mm) of rain falls on Aswan, Egypt. In the country's sunniest and southernmost city, summer temperatures can reach a blistering 114°F (46°C). Aswan is located on the west bank of the Nile River, and it has a very busy marketplace that is also popular with tourists. The Aswan High Dam, at 12,565 feet (3,830 m) long, is the city's most famous landmark. It produces the majority of Egypt's power in the form of hydroelectricity.

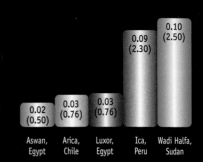

Driest Inhabited Places

Average annual rainfall, in inches (millimeters)

Aswan, Egypt	Arica, Chile	Luxor, Egypt	Ica, Peru	Wadi Halfa, Sudan
0.02 (0.50)	0.03 (0.76)	0.03 (0.76)	0.09 (2.30)	0.10 (2.50)

Place with the Fastest Winds

BARROW ISLAND

On April 12, 1996, Cyclone Olivia blew through Barrow Island in Australia and created a wind gust that reached 253 miles (407 km) an hour. Barrow Island is about 30 miles (48 km) off the coast of Western Australia and is home to many endangered species, such as dugongs and green turtles. The dry, sandy land measures about 78 square miles (202 sq km) and is the second-largest island in Western Australia. Barrow Island also has hundreds of oil wells and is a top source of oil for the country. The island has produced more than 300 million barrels of oil since 1967.

Places with the Fastest Winds

Speed of strongest winds, in miles (kilometers) per hour

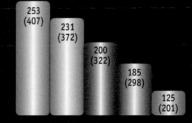

Barrow Island, Australia	Mount Washington, New Hampshire, USA	Commonwealth Bay, Antarctica	South Pole, Antarctica	New Orleans, Louisiana, USA
253 (407)	231 (372)	200 (322)	185 (298)	125 (201)

Tallest Cactus

SAGUARO

Many saguaro cacti grow to a height of 50 feet (15 m), but some have actually reached 75 feet (23 m). That's taller than a seven-story building. Saguaros start out quite small and grow very slowly. A saguaro only reaches about 1 inch (2.5 cm) high during its first 10 years. It will not bloom until it is between 50 and 75 years old. By this time, the cactus has a strong root system that can support about 9–10 tons (8–9 t) of growth. Its spines can measure up to 2.5 inches (5 cm) long. Saguaro cacti live for about 170 years. The giant cacti can be found from southeastern California to southern Arizona.

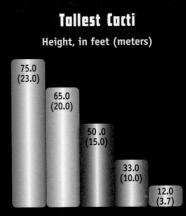

Tallest Cacti

Height, in feet (meters)

Saguaro	Cardon	Organ Pipe	Opuntia	Cane Cholla
75.0 (23.0)	65.0 (20.0)	50.0 (15.0)	33.0 (10.0)	12.0 (3.7)

Tallest Tree
CALIFORNIA REDWOOD

Growing in both California and southern Oregon, California redwoods can reach a height of 385 feet (117 m). Their trunks can grow up to 25 feet (8 m) in diameter. The tallest redwood on record is more than 60 feet (18 m) taller than the Statue of Liberty. Amazingly, this giant tree grows from a seed the size of a tomato. Some redwoods are believed to be more than 2,000 years old. The trees' thick bark and foliage protect them from natural hazards such as insects and fires.

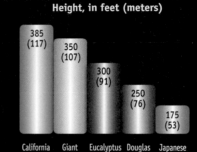

Tallest Trees

Height, in feet (meters)

California Redwood	Giant Sequoia	Eucalyptus	Douglas Fir	Japanese Cedar
385 (117)	350 (107)	300 (91)	250 (76)	175 (53)

Most Poisonous Mushroom

DEATH CAP

Death cap mushrooms are members of the Amanita family, which are among the most dangerous mushrooms in the world. The death cap contains deadly peptide toxins that cause rapid loss of bodily fluids and intense thirst. Within six hours, the poison shuts down the kidneys, liver, and central nervous system, causing coma and—in more than 50 percent of cases—death. Estimates of the number of poisonous mushroom species range from 80 to 2,000. Most experts agree, however, that at least 100 varieties will cause severe symptoms and even death if eaten.

Some of the Most Poisonous Mushrooms

Risk of fatality if consumed

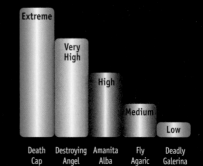

Death Cap	Destroying Angel	Amanita Alba	Fly Agaric	Deadly Galerina
Extreme	Very High	High	Medium	Low

Largest Flower
RAFFLESIA

The blossoms of the giant rafflesia—or "stinking corpse lily"—can reach 36 inches (91 cm) in diameter and weigh up to 25 pounds (11 kg). Its petals can grow 1.5 feet (0.5 m) long and 1 inch (2.5 cm) thick. There are 16 different species of rafflesia. This endangered plant is found only in the rain forests of Borneo and Sumatra. It lives inside the bark of host vines and is noticeable only when its flowers break through to blossom. The large, reddish purple flowers give off a smell similar to rotting meat, which attracts insects that help spread the rafflesia's pollen.

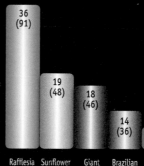

Largest Flowers

Size, in inches (centimeters)

Rafflesia	Sunflower	Giant Water Lily	Brazilian Dutchman	Magnolia
36 (91)	19 (48)	18 (46)	14 (36)	10 (25)

Deadliest Plant

CASTOR BEAN

The castor bean plant produces seeds that contain a protein called ricin. Scientists estimate that ricin is about 6,000 times more poisonous than cyanide and 12,000 times more poisonous than rattlesnake venom. It would take a particle of ricin only about the size of a grain of sand to kill a 160-pound (73 kg) adult. The deadly beans are actually quite pretty and are sometimes used in jewelry. Castor bean plants grow in warmer climates and can reach a height of about 10 feet (3 m). Their leaves can measure up to 2 feet (0.6 m) wide.

Some of the Deadliest Plants

Risk of fatality if consumed

Castor Bean	Rosary Bead	Foxglove	Azalea	English Ivy
Extreme	High	High	Medium	Low

Largest Seed
COCO DE MER

Measuring 3 feet (1 m) in diameter and 12 inches (30 cm) in length, the giant, dark brown seed of the coco de mer palm tree can weigh up to 40 pounds (18 kg). Only a few thousand seeds are produced each year. Coco de mer trees are found on the island of Praslin in the Seychelles Archipelago of the Indian Ocean. The area where some of the few remaining trees grow has been declared a Natural World Heritage Site in an effort to protect the species from poachers looking for the rare seeds. The tree can grow up to 100 feet (31 m) tall, with leaves measuring 20 feet (6 m) long and 12 feet (3.6 m) wide.

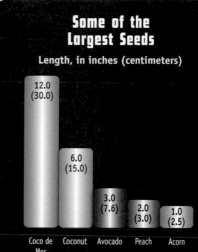

Some of the Largest Seeds

Length, in inches (centimeters)

Coco de Mer	Coconut	Avocado	Peach	Acorn
12.0 (30.0)	6.0 (15.0)	3.0 (7.6)	2.0 (3.0)	1.0 (2.5)

Highest Tsunami Wave Since 1900

LITUYA BAY

A 1,720-foot (524 m) tsunami wave crashed down in Lituya Bay, Alaska, on July 9, 1958. Located in Glacier Bay National Park, the tsunami was caused by a massive landslide that was triggered by an 8.3-magnitude earthquake. The water from the bay covered 5 square miles (13 sq km) of land and traveled inland as far as 3,600 feet (1,097 m). Millions of trees were washed away. Amazingly, because the area was very isolated and the coastline was sheltered by coves, only two people died when their fishing boat sank.

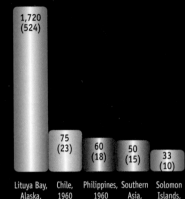

Highest Tsunami Waves Since 1900

Height of wave, in feet (meters)

- 1,720 (524) — Lituya Bay, Alaska, USA, 1958
- 75 (23) — Chile, 1960
- 60 (18) — Philippines, 1960
- 50 (15) — Southern Asia, 2004
- 33 (10) — Solomon Islands, 2007

Most Intense Earthquake Since 1900
CHILE

An explosive earthquake measuring 9.5 on the Richter scale rocked the coast of Chile on May 22, 1960. This is equal to the intensity of about 60,000 hydrogen bombs. Some 2,000 people were killed and another 3,000 injured. The death toll was fairly low because the foreshocks frightened people into the streets. When the massive jolt came, many of the buildings that collapsed were already empty. The coastal towns of Valdivia and Puerto Montt suffered the most damage because they were closest to the epicenter— located about 100 miles (161 km) offshore. On February 27, 2010, Chile was rocked by another huge earthquake (8.8 magnitude), but the loss of life and property was much less than from previous quakes.

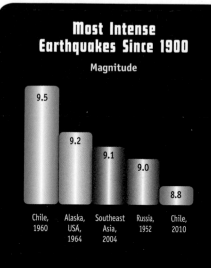

Most Intense Earthquakes Since 1900

Magnitude

Chile, 1960	Alaska, USA, 1964	Southeast Asia, 2004	Russia, 1952	Chile, 2010
9.5	9.2	9.1	9.0	8.8

Most Destructive Flood Since 1900

HURRICANE KATRINA

The pounding rain and storm surges of Hurricane Katrina resulted in catastrophic flooding that cost about $60 billion. The storm formed in late August 2005 over the Bahamas, moved across Florida, and finally hit Louisiana on August 29 as a category-three storm. The storm surge from the Gulf of Mexico flooded the state, as well as neighboring Alabama and Mississippi. Many levees could not hold back the massive amounts of water, and entire towns were destroyed. In total, some 1,800 people lost their lives.

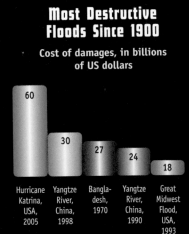

Most Destructive Floods Since 1900

Cost of damages, in billions of US dollars

60	30	27	24	18
Hurricane Katrina, USA, 2005	Yangtze River, China, 1998	Bangladesh, 1970	Yangtze River, China, 1990	Great Midwest Flood, USA, 1993

Worst Oil Spill

GULF WAR

During the Gulf War in 1991, Iraqi troops opened valves of oil wells in Kuwait, releasing more than 240 million gallons (908 million L) of oil into the Persian Gulf. At its worst, the spill measured 101 miles by 42 miles (163 km by 68 km) and was about 5 inches (13 cm) thick. Some of the oil eventually evaporated, another 1 million barrels were collected out of the water, and the rest washed ashore. Although much of the oil can no longer be seen, most of it remains, soaked into the deeper layers of sand along the coast. Amazingly, the wildlife that lives in these areas were not harmed as much as was initially feared. However, salt marsh areas without strong currents were hit the hardest, as oil collected there and killed off entire ecosystems.

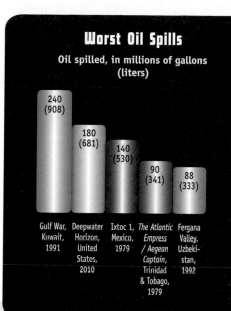

Worst Oil Spills

Oil spilled, in millions of gallons (liters)

240 (908)	180 (681)	140 (530)	90 (341)	88 (333)
Gulf War, Kuwait, 1991	Deepwater Horizon, United States, 2010	Ixtoc 1, Mexico, 1979	The Atlantic Empress / Aegean Captain, Trinidad & Tobago, 1979	Fergana Valley, Uzbekistan, 1992

Most Destructive Tornado Since 1900

OKLAHOMA CITY

On May 3, 1999, a devastating tornado swept through downtown Oklahoma City, Oklahoma, killing 36 people and causing more than $1.2 billion in damages. This powerful twister traveled almost 38 miles (61 km) in four hours and measured 1 mile (1.6 km) wide at times. With raging winds reaching 318 miles (512 km) per hour, it was the strongest wind speed ever recorded. More than 800 houses were destroyed in Oklahoma City alone. Because of the mass destruction caused by this twister, it was classified as a 5—the second-highest possible rating—on the Fujita Tornado Scale.

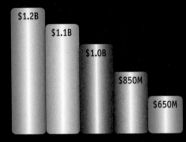

Most Destructive Tornadoes Since 1900

Cost of damages, in US dollars

Oklahoma City, Oklahoma, 1999	Omaha, Nebraska, 1975	Missouri, Illinois, Indiana, 1925	Southern United States, 2008	Southern United States, 2006
$1.2B	$1.1B	$1.0B	$850M	$650M

Devastation from
Hurricane Camille

Most Intense Hurricanes Since 1900

HURRICANE ALLEN &
HURRICANE CAMILLE

Both Hurricane Allen and Hurricane
Camille were category 5 storms
with winds that gusted up to 190 miles
(306 km) per hour. Hurricane Camille
made landfall in the United States along
the mouth of the Mississippi River on
August 17, 1969. Mississippi and Virginia
sustained the most damage, and the
total storm damages cost $1.42 billion.
Hurricane Allen sustained its strongest
winds near Puerto Rico on August 5,
1980. The storm traveled through the
Caribbean, Cuba, the Yucatan Peninsula,
and the south-central United States.
The damages totaled about $1 billion.

Most Intense
Hurricanes Since 1900

**Highest sustained wind speed,
in miles (kilometers) per hour**

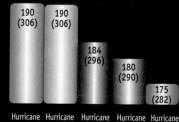

190 (306)	190 (306)	184 (296)	180 (290)	175 (282)
Hurricane Allen, 1980	Hurricane Camille, 1969	Hurricane Gilbert, 1988	Hurricane Mitch, 1998	Hurricane Katrina, 2005

Country that Consumes the Most Coffee

FINLAND

Per capita consumption of coffee in Finland works out to about 1,500 cups of coffee per year, which is an average of more than 4 cups a day. It also means that this small European country brews up about 498 million gallons (2,194 L) annually. Most Finns prefer a strong brew and drink it without cream or sugar. Finland's two main coffee companies are Paulig and Meira. Coffee is the second most valuable commodity in the world (behind oil) and generates about $60 billion annually.

Countries that Consume the Most Coffee

Annual per capita consumption, in cups

Finland	Norway	Sweden	Denmark	Switzerland
1,500	1,260	1,230	1,185	885

Country that Drinks the Most Juice

CANADA

Canadians, on average, drink about 10.8 gallons (40.8 L) of fruit and vegetable juice each year. Kids ages 1 to 3 drink the highest percentage, with about 60 percent consuming juice every day. About 50 percent of kids 18 and under consume some type of juice at least once a day. In fact, kids and teens are three times more likely to choose juice over soda. Canadian juice companies are continually introducing new flavors and products to meet the demand. More sophisticated juices are now marketed to the 18–24 age group, including wild citrus, summit berry, and orange carrot.

Countries that Drink the Most Juice

Annual per capita consumption, in gallons (liters)

Canada	Netherlands	Poland	Germany	Slovenia
10.8 (40.8)	9.6 (36.3)	9.1 (34.4)	8.9 (33.6)	8.3 (31.4)

207

Country that Chews the Most Gum

UNITED STATES

Americans chew a lot of gum! Each year, they go through about 218,500 tons (198,219 t) of the sticky stuff. That averages out to more than 1.5 pounds (0.7 kg) for every person in the country! Gum is the fastest-growing sector in the candy market, increasing by about 7 percent every year. There are more than 1,000 types of gum sold in the United States. Spearmint, peppermint, and cinnamon are among the most popular flavors. Gum is gaining in popularity as people look for more low-calorie treats to enjoy.

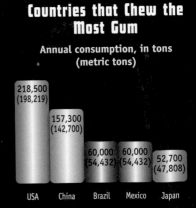

Countries that Chew the Most Gum

Annual consumption, in tons (metric tons)

USA	218,500 (198,219)
China	157,300 (142,700)
Brazil	60,000 (54,432)
Mexico	60,000 (54,432)
Japan	52,700 (47,808)

Country that Eats the Most Chocolate

UNITED KINGDOM

On average, each citizen of the United Kingdom eats about 25.4 pounds (11.5 kg) of chocolate annually. The UK enjoys a combined total of 1.56 billion pounds (707 million kg) each year, which accounts for about 30 percent of the chocolate eaten in all of Europe. Bar chocolate, such as Snickers and a local Crunchie brand, accounts for about 45 percent of all sales. Dark chocolate sales have also increased recently due to reports that it is healthier than milk and white chocolate.

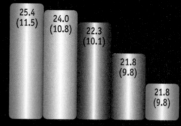

Countries that Eat the Most Chocolate

Annual per capita consumption, in pounds (kilograms)

UK	Liechten-stein	Luxembourg	Ireland	Switzerland
25.4 (11.5)	24.0 (10.8)	22.3 (10.1)	21.8 (9.8)	21.8 (9.8)

Country that Consumes the Most Ice Cream

AUSTRALIA

Each person in Australia eats about 31.7 pints (15.0 L) of ice cream annually. That means the country demolishes more than 83.2 million gallons (314.9 million L) each year. The country's favorite flavors are vanilla, chocolate, and strawberry. Residents of New South Wales eat ice cream the most often—about 5.5 times a month—followed by residents of Queensland at 5.2 times a month. Each year, the Australian ice-cream market takes in approximately $391.4 million and employs about 1,100 people.

Countries that Consume the Most Ice Cream

Annual per capita consumption, in pints (liters)

Australia	USA	Nauru	New Zealand	Canada
31.7 (15.0)	26.0 (12.3)	25.3 (11.9)	23.4 (11.1)	22.7 (10.7)

Country that Eats the Most Meat
NAURU

Each person in Nauru eats an average of 269 pounds (122 kg) of meat annually. Nauru is a small island in the South Pacific, just north of the Solomon Islands. There are several different nationalities that make up the island's culture, including Chinese and Vietnamese, so the cooking methods and recipes are varied. Cured meats and smoked ham are very popular in traditional dishes. Canned meat is one of the most popular items in local grocery stores. The high meat consumption is unfortunately contributing to rising levels of obesity and diabetes.

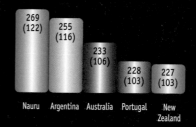

Countries that Eat the Most Meat

Annual per capita consumption, in pounds (kilograms)

Nauru	Argentina	Australia	Portugal	New Zealand
269 (122)	255 (116)	233 (106)	228 (103)	227 (103)

Country that Eats the Most Fast Food

UNITED STATES

Each person in the United States spends about $595 a year on fast food. That means that an average family of four shells out $2,380 a year for burgers, fries, and other menu items. As the economy remains weak, more families are choosing fast-food meals over sit-down restaurants. There are about 200,000 fast-food restaurants in the country, and they take in a combined $120 billion each year. Some of the most popular restaurants include McDonald's, Wendy's, Subway, Burger King, and Taco Bell. Many of these restaurants are following the trend toward healthier eating and putting more nutritious items on their menus.

Countries that Eat the Most Fast Food

Annual per capita spending, in US dollars

USA	Canada	Ireland	UK	Australia
595	551	526	441	420

Country that Recycles the Most Steel
BELGIUM

Belgium recycles 93 percent of its steel packaging, including food cans and aerosol containers. This is 24 percent higher than the world's steel can recycling rate. Steel's magnetic properties make it easier to recycle than other metals, since it can be sorted by magnets instead of by hand. It also does not lose strength when it is processed, so it can be recycled over and over again. Recycling steel reduces the need for mining and cuts down on carbon dioxide emissions. Recycling steel uses about 75 percent less energy than producing steel from raw materials.

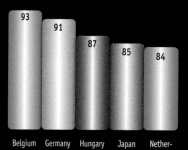

Countries that Recycle the Most Steel

Percentage of steel that is recycled

Belgium	Germany	Hungary	Japan	Netherlands
93	91	87	85	84

MONEY RECORDS

Most Expensive/Valuable · Bestsellers
Companies & Consumption

Most Expensive Restaurant

MASA

At this elegant Japanese restaurant, diners will enjoy a meal with an average cost of $400. Located in Manhattan's Time Warner Building, Masa has just 26 seats. There are no menus here because the sushi chef—Masayoshi Takayama—prepares only what specialties are in season. Diners start with 5 appetizers, followed by a sushi entrée with at least 15 different types of seafood flown in from Japan. Masa opened in 2004 and serves lunch and dinner. If restaurant-goers would like to save a little money, Bar Masa is located next door and offers much more economical meals.

Most Expensive Restaurants

Average cost of a meal, in US dollars

400	395	375	360	270
Masa, New York City, USA	L'Arpège, Paris, France	Aragawa, Tokyo, Japan	Joel Rubuchon at the Mansion, Las Vegas, USA	El Bulli, Roses, Spain

Most Valuable Baseball

MARK MCGWIRE'S 70TH HOME-RUN BASEBALL

Mark McGwire's 70th home-run baseball fetched $3.05 million at auction in January 1999. The bid, which was actually $2.7 million plus a large commission fee, is the most money paid for a sports artifact. The ball was only expected to sell for about $1 million. Businessman and baseball fan Todd McFarlane said he bought the ball because he wanted to own a piece of history. This famous baseball marked the end of the exciting 1998 home-run race between Mark McGwire and Sammy Sosa. Both beat Roger Maris's three-decade record of 61—Sosa with 66 and McGwire with 70.

Most Valuable Baseballs

Price paid at auction, in US dollars

3.05M				
	805,000	752,467	650,000	517,500
Mark McGwire's 70th of Season	Babe Ruth's 1st All-Star Game Home Run	Barry Bonds' 756th	Hank Aaron's 755th	Barry Bonds' 73rd of Season

Todd McFarlane

Most Valuable Production Car

KOENIGSEGG TREVITA

The Koenigsegg Trevita sells for more than $2.21 million—more than 80 times the cost of an average car. The superpricey sports car is based on the Koenigsegg CCXR. With a 5.0 liter twin supercharged V8 engine, the Trevita has a top speed of 250 miles (402 km) per hour. It can go from 0 to 62 miles (100 km) per hour in just 2.9 seconds. Since the Trevita is made out of a shiny, diamond-coated carbon fiber, it was given a name that means "three whites" in Swedish. And as the name suggests, only three of these cars will be produced.

Most Valuable Production Cars

Price, in millions of US dollars

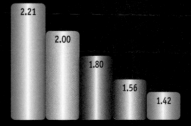

Koenigsegg Trevita	Bugatti Veyron 16.4 Grand Sport	Pagani Zonda Cinque Roadster	Lamborghini Reventón Roadster	Lamborghini Reventón
2.21	2.00	1.80	1.56	1.42

217

Largest Global Retailer

WAL-MART

Megadiscount retail chain Wal-Mart had more than $405 billion in sales during 2009. Wal-Mart serves more than 200 million customers each week at its more than 8,000 stores. Located in 15 countries, the company employs more than 1.4 million people in the United States and another 600,000 worldwide. This makes Wal-Mart the largest private employer in North America. Wal-Mart also believes in giving back to the community and has donated more than $400 million to local charities since it opened its doors in 1962. Wal-Mart is currently ranked number two in the Fortune 500 list of most profitable companies.

Largest Global Retailers
2009 sales, in billions of US dollars

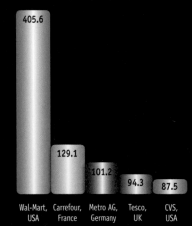

Wal-Mart, USA	Carrefour, France	Metro AG, Germany	Tesco, UK	CVS, USA
405.6	129.1	101.2	94.3	87.5

Top Internet Retailer
AMAZON.COM

Amazon.com rules the Internet with $14.8 billion in sales. Amazon was founded by Jeff Bezos and began selling books in July 1995. It slowly added different types of merchandise to its virtual shelves and now has 12 different departments, including toys, music, electronics, home and garden, and sports. In addition to donating to various charities, Amazon is concerned about the environment. The company has greatly reduced packaging material since 1997, and ships items in boxes that are 100 percent recyclable.

Top Internet Retailers
2009 internet sales, in billions of US dollars

Amazon.com	14.8
Staples	5.6
Office Depot	4.9
Dell	4.2
HP Home & Home Office Store	3.4

United States' Bestselling Automobiles
FORD F-SERIES

Ford sold 413,625 F-Series trucks during 2009. The F-Series originated in 1948, when the F-1 (half-ton), the F-2 (three-quarter-ton), and the F-3 (Heavy Duty) were introduced. Since then, many modifications and new editions have been introduced, including the F-150. The modern F-150 sports a V8 engine and the option of a regular, extended, or crew cab. The bed size ranges from 5.5 feet (1.6 m) to 8 feet (2.4 km). The Platinum F-150—the top-of-the-line version—features platinum chrome wheels, a fancy grille design, leather upholstery, and heated seats.

United States' Bestselling Automobiles

Number of automobiles sold in 2009

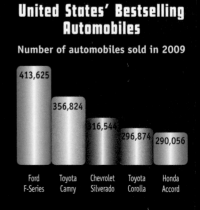

Ford F-Series	Toyota Camry	Chevrolet Silverado	Toyota Corolla	Honda Accord
413,625	356,824	316,544	296,874	290,056

Most Profitable Company
EXXONMOBIL

With profits of $45.2 billion, gasoline giant ExxonMobil is the world's most profitable company. ExxonMobil produces, transports, and sells crude oil and natural gas worldwide. It also manufactures and sells petroleum products across the globe. Its Mobil 1 synthetic motor oil is the world's leading brand. ExxonMobil has 40 oil refineries in 20 countries and is capable of producing 6.4 million barrels of oil each day. They provide fuel to about 35,000 service stations, some 700 airports, and more than 200 ports.

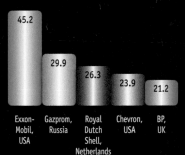

Most Profitable Companies

2009 profits, in billions of US dollars

Exxon-Mobil, USA	45.2
Gazprom, Russia	29.9
Royal Dutch Shell, Netherlands	26.3
Chevron, USA	23.9
BP, UK	21.2

Exxon Regular
Unleaded
$ Price per gallon
All taxes included
MINIMUM OCTANE RATING
(R+M) / 2 METHOD
87 PRESS

Exxon Plus
Unleaded
$ Price per gallon
All taxes included
MINIMUM OCTANE RATING
(R+M) / 2 METHOD
89 PRESS

Exxon Supreme
Unleaded
$ Price per gallon
All taxes included
MINIMUM OCTANE RATING
(R+M) / 2 METHOD
91 PRESS

WARNING
HAZARD OF OVERFILL

Country that Spends the Most on Toys

UNITED KINGDOM

On average, each person in the United Kingdom spends more than $184 on toys every year. That's about $11.2 billion annually. The ever-growing market is driven mostly by video games, since about 37 percent of people aged 16 to 49 describe themselves as active gamers. Some of the most popular items include the Sony PlayStation 3 and the Nintendo Wii. The two major companies selling toys in the United Kingdom are Mattel and Hasbro, both based in the United States. Some smaller local companies include Vivid Imaginations and Hornby.

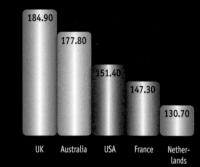

Countries that Spend the Most on Toys

Annual per capita spending, in US dollars

UK	184.90
Australia	177.80
USA	151.40
France	147.30
Netherlands	130.70

Largest Global Food Franchise
SUBWAY

Subway has 33,038 franchises spread throughout 90 countries. The original shop was founded in 1965 as Pete's Super Submarines in Connecticut, and started franchising as Subway in 1974. It has steadily surpassed all other food franchises since then, partly because it is considered a healthier alternative to other fast-food restaurants. In the United States, Subway serves about 2,800 sandwiches and salads every minute. There are more than 2 million different sandwich combinations on the menu, but the most popular choices are the Turkey Breast, the Italian BMT, and the Subway Club.

Largest Global Food Franchises

Number of franchises

Subway	McDonald's	KFC	Pizza Hut	Burger King
33,038	32,158	15,580	13,175	12,000

HUMAN-MADE RECORDS

Structures · Travel · Transportation

Amusement Park with the Most Rides

CEDAR POINT

Located in Sandusky, Ohio, Cedar Point offers park visitors 74 rides to enjoy. Skyhawk—the park's newest ride—thrusts riders 125 feet (38 m) into the air and is the largest swing ride in the world. Top Thrill Dragster roller coaster is the second tallest in the world at 420 feet (128 m). And with 17 roller coasters, Cedar Point also has the most coasters of any theme park in the world. Over 53,963 feet (16,448 m) of coaster track—more than 10 miles (16.1 km)—run through the park. In 2008, Cedar Point was named "Best Amusement Park in the World" by *Amusement Today* for the eleventh time.

Amusement Parks with the Most Rides

Number of rides

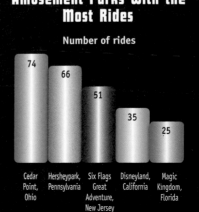

Cedar Point, Ohio	Hersheypark, Pennsylvania	Six Flags Great Adventure, New Jersey	Disneyland, California	Magic Kingdom, Florida
74	66	51	35	25

City with the Most Skyscrapers

HONG KONG

A total of 202 skyscrapers rises high above the streets of Hong Kong. In fact, the world's fifth-tallest building—Two International Finance Centre—towers 1,362 feet (415 m) above the city. Because this bustling Chinese business center has only about 160 square miles (414 sq km) of land suitable for building, architects have to build up instead of out. And Hong Kong keeps growing—60 of the city's giant buildings were constructed in the last seven years. Some large development projects, such as the Sky Tower Apartment Complex, added seven skyscrapers to the landscape in just one year.

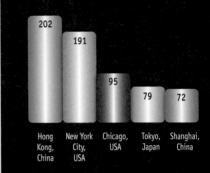

Cities with the Most Skyscrapers

Number of skyscrapers

Hong Kong, China	New York City, USA	Chicago, USA	Tokyo, Japan	Shanghai, China
202	191	95	79	72

Tallest Apartment Building

Q1

Q1, a luxury apartment complex on Australia's Gold Coast, rises 1,058 feet (323 m) above the surrounding sand. There are 526 apartments within the building's 80 floors. Some apartments have glass-enclosed balconies. Q1 residents can enjoy Australia's only beachside observation deck and a 10-story sky garden. Some other amenities include retail outlets, a lagoon swimming pool, a spa, a sauna, and a fitness center. And just in case all nine elevators are out of order, there are 1,430 steps from the penthouse to the basement!

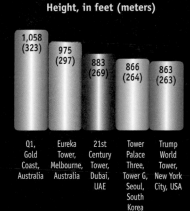

Tallest Apartment Buildings

Height, in feet (meters)

Q1, Gold Coast, Australia	Eureka Tower, Melbourne, Australia	21st Century Tower, Dubai, UAE	Tower Palace Three, Tower G, Seoul, South Korea	Trump World Tower, New York City, USA
1,058 (323)	975 (297)	883 (269)	866 (264)	863 (263)

227

Largest Dome

02

Located in London, UK, the 02 has a roof that measures 1,050 feet (320 m) in diameter and covers 861,113 square feet (80,000 sq m). That's large enough to contain the Great Pyramid of Giza! The roof is made of 107,639 square feet (10,000 sq m) of fabric and is held up by 43 miles of steel cable. The dome is currently being used as a concert venue, hosting such acts as Bon Jovi, Rihanna, and Aerosmith. It also boasts a movie complex, theaters, and restaurants. The dome was built for the country's millennium celebration. After the New Year's celebration, renovations began to turn the dome into a sports complex, and it will be used for the 2012 Olympics.

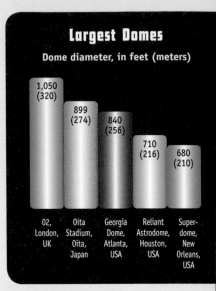

Largest Domes

Dome diameter, in feet (meters)

1,050 (320)	899 (274)	840 (256)	710 (216)	680 (210)
02, London, UK	Oita Stadium, Oita, Japan	Georgia Dome, Atlanta, USA	Reliant Astrodome, Houston, USA	Super-dome, New Orleans, USA

Tallest Habitable Building

BURJ KHALIFA

The newly constructed Burj Khalifa in the United Arab Emirates towers 2,684 feet (818 m) above the ground. With 110 floors, the building cost about $4.1 billion to construct. Both a hotel and apartments are housed inside the luxury building, which covers 500 acres (202 ha). The building will feature the world's fastest elevators, traveling at a speed of 40 miles (64 km) an hour. The tower supplies its occupants with about 250,000 gallons (66,043 L) of water a day, and will deliver enough electricity to power 360,000 100-watt lightbulbs.

Tallest Habitable Buildings

Height, in feet (meters)

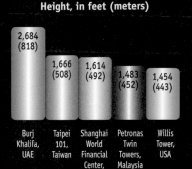

2,684 (818)	1,666 (508)	1,614 (492)	1,483 (452)	1,454 (443)
Burj Khalifa, UAE	Taipei 101, Taiwan	Shanghai World Financial Center, China	Petronas Twin Towers, Malaysia	Willis Tower, USA

Largest Mall
SOUTH CHINA MALL

The South China Mall in Dongguan City covers 7.1 million square feet (0.66 million sq m) of retail and entertainment space. The megamall—which opened in 2005—was designed with seven major areas that resemble Amsterdam, Paris, Rome, Venice, Egypt, the Caribbean, and California. And, for shoppers too tired to walk from one end of the giant retail outlet to the other, there are gondolas and water taxis located on the mile-long, human-made canal that circles the perimeter. However, the mall, which was designed to showcase 1,500 stores, only houses about 20. Retailers have been slow to set up shop at the mall.

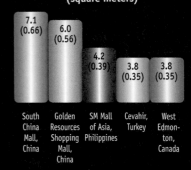

Largest Malls

Area, in millions of square feet (square meters)

South China Mall, China	Golden Resources Shopping Mall, China	SM Mall of Asia, Philippines	Cevahir, Turkey	West Edmonton, Canada
7.1 (0.66)	6.0 (0.56)	4.2 (0.39)	3.8 (0.35)	3.8 (0.35)

Largest Library
LIBRARY OF CONGRESS

The Library of Congress is the largest library in the world, with more than 138 million items on approximately 650 miles (1046 km) of bookshelves. That means that the shelves could stretch from their home in Washington, DC, all the way to Chicago, Illinois! The collections include more than 32 million books and other print materials, 2.9 million recordings, 12.5 million photographs, 5.3 million maps, 5.5 million pieces of sheet music, and 61 million manuscripts. The Library receives about 22,000 items each business day, and adds approximately 10,000 items to the collections daily.

Largest Libraries
Number of books housed, in millions

Library of Congress, USA	British Library, England	Deutsche National-bibliothek, Germany	Library of the Russian Academy of Sciences, Russia	National Library of Canada, Canada
32.1	29.0	22.2	20.5	19.5

Largest Sports Stadium

RUNGRADO MAY FIRST STADIUM

The Rungrado May First Stadium, also known as the May Day Stadium, can seat up to 150,000 people. The interior of the stadium covers 2.2 million square feet (204,386 sq m). Located in Pyongyang, North Korea, this venue is mostly used for soccer matches and other athletic contests. It is named after Rungra Island, on which the stadium is located, in the middle of the Taedong River. When it is not being used for sporting events, the stadium is used for choreographed gymnastics known as Arirang.

Largest Sports Stadiums

Number of seats

Rungrado May First Stadium, North Korea	Salt Lake Stadium, India	Beaver Stadium, USA	Michigan Stadium, USA	Estadio Azteca, Mexico
150,000	120,000	107,282	106,201	105,000

Largest Restaurant

DAMASCUS GATE

With its 6,014 seats, Damascus Gate in Syria is by far the world's largest restaurant. During the busy summer months, the restaurant employs about 1,800 people to staff the 581,250-square-foot (54,000 sq m) dining area and 26,900-square-foot (2,500 sq m) kitchen. The open-air area features both waterfalls and fountains. The kitchen functions like a production line, and a single chef can prepare 25 to 30 servings of popular dishes—such as hummus—in about a minute. That's about one bowl every two seconds!

Largest Restaurants
Number of seats

Damascus Gate, Syria	The Royal Dragon Restaurant, Thailand	Das Dutchman Essenhaus, USA	Macau De Café, Philippines	Café de Macao, China
6,014	5,000	1,100	1,050	1,000

233

Largest Movie Theater

RADIO CITY MUSIC HALL

New York City's Radio City Music Hall is the largest single-screen theater in the world, with 5,933 seats. It's no wonder that the theater has become a hot spot for films. Since 1933, more than 700 movies have opened there, including *Mary Poppins*, *101 Dalmatians*, and *The Lion King*. The massive theater has a marquee that measures a full city block in length, and its auditorium is 160 feet (49 m) long. Its ceilings tower 84 feet (26 m) high. Since it first opened, more than 300 million people have attended shows and films there.

Largest Movie Theaters

Number of seats

Radio City Music Hall, New York City, USA	Fox Theatre, Detroit, USA	Fox Theatre, St. Louis, USA	Cine Teatro Gran Rex, Buenos Aires, Argentina	Opera House, Boston, USA
5,933	5,045	4,500	3,350	2,907

Top Tourist Country

FRANCE

France hosts more than 79 million tourists annually. That's about two and a half times the entire population of Canada! The most popular French destinations are Paris and the Mediterranean coast. In July and August—the most popular months to visit France—tourists flock to the westernmost coastal areas of the region. In the winter, visitors hit the slopes at major ski resorts in the northern Alps. Tourists also visit many of France's world-renowned landmarks and monuments, including the Eiffel Tower, Notre Dame, the Louvre, and the Palace of Versailles. Most tourists are from other European countries, especially Germany.

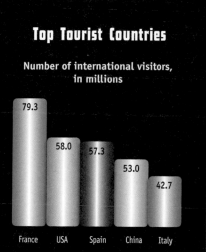

Top Tourist Countries

Number of international visitors, in millions

France	USA	Spain	China	Italy
79.3	58.0	57.3	53.0	42.7

Most Visited City

NEW YORK

New York City hosted more than 45.3 million visitors during 2009. About 8.6 million of those travelers were from overseas. The city that never sleeps offers a wide variety of attractions, including historic buildings and monuments, theater, shopping, museums, and world-class restaurants. Many events draw tourists as well, such as the Macy's Thanksgiving Day Parade and New Year's Eve in Times Square. There were about 23.6 million nights booked at the city's 81,500 hotel rooms in 2009, bringing in more than $315 million in revenue. New York City's thriving tourism industry employs more than 311,000 people.

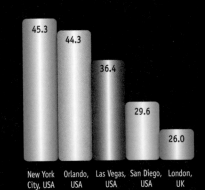

Most Visited Cities

Number of annual visitors, in millions

New York City, USA	Orlando, USA	Las Vegas, USA	San Diego, USA	London, UK
45.3	44.3	36.4	29.6	26.0

United States' Most Visited National Park

GREAT SMOKY MOUNTAINS NATIONAL PARK

Almost 9.5 million visitors enjoyed the beauty of Great Smoky Mountains National Park during 2009. Spread between Tennessee and North Carolina, the park covers more than 521,085 acres (210,875 ha) and features 16 mountain peaks with elevations above 6,000 feet (1,829 m). There are more than 800 miles (1,287 km) of hiking trails throughout the park, which give visitors a chance to glimpse some of the bears, deer, elks, and other wildlife that live in the Great Smoky Mountains. More than 240 species of birds have been found in the park, and 60 of them live there year-round.

United States' Most Visited National Parks

Number of annual visitors, in millions

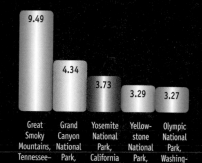

Great Smoky Mountains, Tennessee–North Carolina	Grand Canyon National Park, Arizona	Yosemite National Park, California	Yellow-stone National Park, Wyoming–Montana–Idaho	Olympic National Park, Washington
9.49	4.34	3.73	3.29	3.27

Country with the Most Airports

UNITED STATES

There are 15,095 airports located in the United States. That is more than the number of airports for the other nine top countries combined. The top two busiest airports in the world are also located in the United States. Altogether, US airports serve more than 709 million domestic travelers a year. With the threat of terrorism and the state of the economy, the airline industry lost $10 billion in 2002. In September 2005, rising fuel costs and competition from discount airlines caused several major airlines to file for bankruptcy. Since that time, the airline industry has seen limited growth and profits, mainly due to the country's sluggish economy.

Countries with the Most Airports

Number of airports

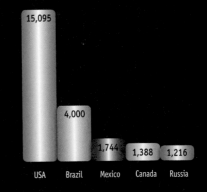

USA	Brazil	Mexico	Canada	Russia
15,095	4,000	1,744	1,388	1,216

Busiest Airport

HARTSFIELD-JACKSON ATLANTA INTERNATIONAL AIRPORT

The Hartsfield-Jackson Atlanta International Airport serves more than 90 million travelers in one year. That's more people than are living in California, Texas, and Florida combined. Approximately 967,050 planes depart and arrive at this airport every year. With parking lots, runways, maintenance facilities, and other buildings, the Hartsfield terminal complex covers about 130 acres (53 ha). Hartsfield-Jackson Atlanta International Airport has a north and a south terminal, an underground train, and six concourses with a total of 154 domestic and 28 international gates.

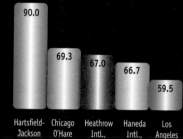

Busiest Airports

Number of annual passengers, in millions

Hartsfield-Jackson Atlanta Intl., USA	Chicago O'Hare Intl., USA	Heathrow Intl., UK	Haneda Intl., Japan	Los Angeles Intl., USA
90.0	69.3	67.0	66.7	59.5

Busiest Airline

SOUTHWEST AIRLINES

When travelers took to the skies in 2009, 101.3 million of them chose to fly Southwest Airlines. The company flies to 68 US cities, with approximately 3,100 flights a day. With a fleet of 530 Boeing 737 planes—each an average of about nine years old—Southwest also has some of the newest planes in the industry. The company was founded in 1971 and only offered service within Texas. By 1982, service was expanded to major cities throughout the country, including San Francisco, Los Angeles, and Phoenix. Today, Southwest employs more than 35,000 people throughout the country.

Busiest Airlines

Number of annual passengers, in millions

Southwest Airlines	American Airlines	Delta Airlines	China Southern Airlines	United Airlines
101.3	85.7	67.7	66.0	56.0

Country that Produces the Most Cars

JAPAN

Japan produces close to 10 million cars annually—that's almost enough to give every man, woman, and child living in Michigan one vehicle. Japan began producing cars in the early 1900s, and became the world's top producer by 2000. The country has about 12 main automakers, including Toyota, Honda, Nissan, Mitsubishi, Subaru, and Isuzu. However, with the economic crisis worsening in 2009, Japan—along with many other countries—has cut auto jobs and slowed production to save money.

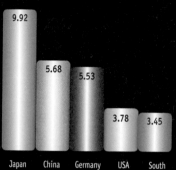

Countries that Produce the Most Cars

Number of cars produced annually, in millions

Japan	China	Germany	USA	South Korea
9.92	5.68	5.53	3.78	3.45

Times Sq-42 St
Station
S N Q R W
1 2 3 7
♿ Elevator to N O R W at 42 St
For A C E enter at 8 Avenue

Enter with or buy MetroCard
6am-12 midnight or see
agent at 42 St & 7 Av

City with the Longest Subway System
NEW YORK CITY

The New York subway system consists of 660 miles (1,062.2 km) of track—more than enough to run from the Big Apple to Louisville, Kentucky. An additional 182 miles (292.9 km) of track lie beneath the city streets, but they are not currently in use. New York City has 468 subway stations, which is just 35 fewer than the number of all other US stations combined. There are approximately 6,485 subway cars in use, and together they travel about 342.5 million miles (569.2 million km) annually. The New York City subway system opened in 1904 with 9 miles (14.5 km) of track and charged just five cents per ride.

Cities with the Longest Subway Systems

Subway length, in miles (kilometers)

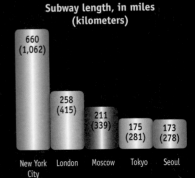

New York City	London	Moscow	Tokyo	Seoul
660 (1,062)	258 (415)	211 (339)	175 (281)	173 (278)

City with the Busiest Subway System

TOKYO

Every year, almost 3 billion riders pack into the Tokyo subway. The system operates more than 2,500 cars and 282 subway stations. The tracks run for 175 miles (281 km). The Tokyo Underground Railroad opened in 1927. It has expanded through the years to include nine subway lines that connect the bustling areas of Chiyoda, Minato, and Chuo. The Tokyo Metro has recently taken steps to upgrade its cars and stations, reinforcing car frames and redesigning station platforms.

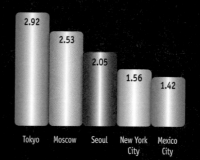

Cities with the Busiest Subway Systems

Number of passengers per year, in billions

City	Passengers (billions)
Tokyo	2.92
Moscow	2.53
Seoul	2.05
New York City	1.56
Mexico City	1.42

Country with the Most Vehicles Per Capita
UNITED STATES

With 793 motor vehicles for every 1,000 people, the United States has more passenger cars and trucks per capita than any other country. There are only 682 licensed drivers per 1,000 people, so available cars outnumber the people who can drive them. There are approximately 245 million motor vehicles registered in the country. Wyoming has the highest registration per capita with 1,247 vehicles, followed by Iowa with 1,125 and North Dakota with 1,111. However, with the economic slump of 2009, car sales and production dropped from the previous year and are expected to decline again in 2010.

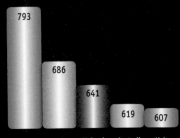

Countries with the Most Vehicles Per Capita

Number of vehicles per 1,000 people

USA	Luxembourg	Malaysia	Australia	Malta
793	686	641	619	607

US RECORDS

Alabama to Wyoming

State with the Oldest Mardi Gras

ALABAMA

People in Mobile, Alabama, have been celebrating Mardi Gras since 1703, although they did not have an official parade event until 1831. After a brief hiatus during the Civil War, the celebrations started back up in 1866 and have been growing ever since. Today, some 100,000 people gather in Mobile to enjoy the 40 parades that take place during the two weeks that lead up to Mardi Gras. On the biggest day—Fat Tuesday—six parades wind through the downtown waterfront, with floats and costumed dancers. But at the stroke of midnight, the partying stops and plans for the next year begin.

United States' Oldest Mardi Gras Celebrations

Number of years since celebration began

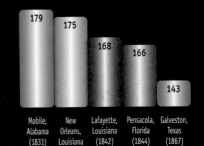

Mobile, Alabama (1831)	New Orleans, Louisiana (1835)	Lafayette, Louisiana (1842)	Pensacola, Florida (1844)	Galveston, Texas (1867)
179	175	168	166	143

*As of 2010

State with the Largest National Forest

ALASKA

The Tongass National Forest covers approximately 16,800,000 acres (6,798,900 ha) in southeast Alaska. That's about the same size as West Virginia. It is also home to the world's largest temperate rain forest. Some of the forest's trees are more than 700 years old. About 11,000 miles (17,703 km) of shoreline are inside the park. Some of the animals that live in the forest include bears, salmon, and wolves. The world's largest concentration of bald eagles also spend the fall and winter here on the Chilkat River.

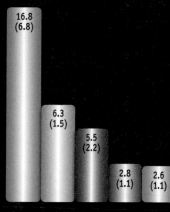

United States' Largest National Forests

Size, in millions of acres (hectares)

Tongass National Forest, Alaska	Humboldt-Toiyabe National Forest, California/Nevada	Chugach National Forest, Alaska	Tonto National Forest, Arizona	Boise National Forest, Idaho
16.8 (6.8)	6.3 (1.5)	5.5 (2.2)	2.8 (1.1)	2.6 (1.1)

State with the Largest Collection of Telescopes

ARIZONA

The Kitt Peak National Observatory is home to 27 different telescopes—25 optical telescopes and 2 radio telescopes. Located above the Sonora Desert, the site was chosen to house the collection of equipment because of its clear weather, low relative humidity, and steady atmosphere. Eight different astronomical research institutions maintain and operate the telescopes. The observatory is overseen by the National Optical Astronomy Observatories. One of the most prominent telescopes housed at Kitt Peak is the McMath-Pierce Solar Telescope, the second-largest solar telescope in the world.

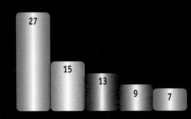

United States' Largest Collections of Telescopes

Number of telescopes

Kitt Peak National Observatory, Arizona	Custer Institute, New York	Mauna Kea, Hawaii	Stull Observatory, New York	Lick Observatory, California
27	15	13	9	7

State that Grows the Most Rice

ARKANSAS

Farmers in Arkansas produced almost 5 million tons (4.5 million t) of rice in 2009, which was about 45 percent of all rice grown in the country. With that harvest, farmers could give every person in the United States 36 pounds (16 kg) of rice and still have a little left over. There are more than 1.48 million acres (598,934 ha) of rice planted across the state, and the crops bring about $1.33 billion in revenue annually. Agriculture is a very important part of Arkansas's economy, employing more than 287,000 workers, or about 20 percent of the state's workforce.

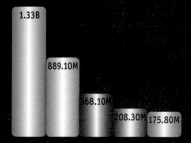

States that Grow the Most Rice

2009 sales, in US dollars

Arkansas	California	Louisiana	Mississippi	Missouri
1.33B	889.10M	368.10M	208.30M	175.80M

State with the World's Largest Laser

CALIFORNIA

The National Ignition Facility in California is home to the NIF laser—the largest laser in the world, weighing 264,000 pounds (119,748 kg) and featuring a target chamber with a 32.8-foot (10 m) diameter. The NIF laser consists of 192 laser beams that can collectively focus on a tiny spot within the target chamber, creating a temperature of 100 million degrees. That's about 60 times more powerful than the next most powerful laser. This will help scientists research new ways to create energy in the future. The giant complex that houses the laser is approximately the size of three football fields.

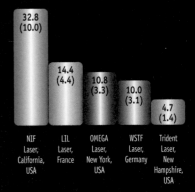

World's Largest Lasers

Diameter of target chamber, in feet (meters)

32.8 (10.0)	14.4 (4.4)	10.8 (3.3)	10.0 (3.1)	4.7 (1.4)
NIF Laser, California, USA	LIL Laser, France	OMEGA Laser, New York, USA	WSTF Laser, Germany	Trident Laser, New Hampshire, USA

State's Baseball Team with the Highest Seasonal Attendance

COLORADO

In 1993, the seasonal attendance for the Colorado Rockies was an impressive 4.48 million fans. The Rockies finished up their inaugural season in October of the same year with the most wins by a National League expansion team. The Rockies played at Mile High Stadium for their first two years. The team moved to Denver's Coors Field in 1995. The new park was designed to have 43,800 seats, but with such high attendance at Mile High Stadium, architects reworked the plans to include 50,200 seats. The team proceeded to sell out 203 consecutive games.

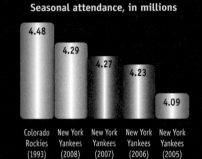

Baseball Teams with the Highest Seasonal Attendance

Seasonal attendance, in millions

Colorado Rockies (1993)	New York Yankees (2008)	New York Yankees (2007)	New York Yankees (2006)	New York Yankees (2005)
4.48	4.29	4.27	4.23	4.09

State with the Oldest Theme Park

CONNECTICUT

Lake Compounce in Bristol, Connecticut, first opened as a picnic park in 1846. The park's first electric roller coaster, the Green Dragon, was introduced in 1914 and cost ten cents per ride. It was replaced by the Wildcat in 1927, and the wooden coaster still operates today. In 1996 the park got a $50 million upgrade, which included the thrilling new roller coaster Boulder Dash. It is the only coaster to be built into a mountainside. Another $3.3 million was spent on upgrades in 2005, including an 800-foot (244 m) lazy river.

United States' Oldest Theme Parks

Number of years open*

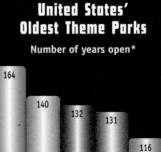

Lake Compounce, Connecticut (1846)	Cedar Point, Ohio (1870)	Idlewild Park, Pennsylvania (1878)	Seabreeze Park, New York (1879)	Lakemont Park, Pennsylvania (1894)
164	140	132	131	116

*As of 2010

State with the Largest Pumpkin-Throwing Contest
DELAWARE

Each year approximately 20,000 people gather in Sussex County, Delaware, for the annual World Championship Punkin Chunkin. More than 60 teams compete during the three-day festival to see who can chuck their pumpkin the farthest. Each team constructs a machine that has a mechanical or compressed-air firing device—no explosives are allowed. The farthest a pumpkin has traveled during the championship is 4,434 feet (1,352 m), or the length of twelve football fields. The total combined distance of all the pumpkins chunked at the 2007 championship totaled almost 12 miles (19 km). Each year the festival raises about $100,000 and benefits St. Jude Children's Hospital.

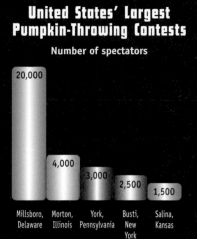

United States' Largest Pumpkin-Throwing Contests
Number of spectators

Location	Spectators
Millsboro, Delaware	20,000
Morton, Illinois	4,000
York, Pennsylvania	3,000
Busti, New York	2,500
Salina, Kansas	1,500

State with the Most Lightning Strikes

FLORIDA

Southern Florida is known as the Lightning Capital of the United States, with 26.3 bolts occurring over each square mile (2.6 sq km)—the equivalent of 10 city blocks—each year. Some 70 percent of all strikes occur between noon and 6:00 p.m., and the most dangerous months are July and August. Most lightning bolts measure 2 to 3 miles (5.2 to 7.8 km) long and can generate between 100 million and 1 billion volts of electricity. The air in a lightning bolt is heated to 50,000°F (27,760°C).

States with the Most Lightning Strikes

Annual bolts per square mile (2.6 sq km)

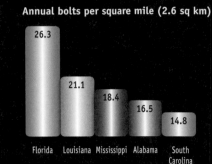

Florida	Louisiana	Mississippi	Alabama	South Carolina
26.3	21.1	18.4	16.5	14.8

State with the Largest Sports Hall of Fame

GEORGIA

The Georgia Sports Hall of Fame fills 43,000 square feet (3,995 sq m) with memorabilia from Georgia's most accomplished college, amateur, and professional athletes. Some 230,000 bricks, 245 tons (222 t) of steel, and 7,591 pounds (3,443 kg) of glass were used in its construction. The hall owns more than 3,000 artifacts and displays about 1,000 of them at a time. Some Hall of Famers include baseball legend Hank Aaron, Olympic basketball great Theresa Edwards, and Super Bowl I champion Bill Curry.

United States' Largest Sports Halls of Fame

Area, in square feet (square meters)

Georgia Sports Hall of Fame	Virginia Sports Hall of Fame	Alabama Sports Hall of Fame	Mississippi Sports Hall of Fame	Kansas Sports Hall of Fame
43,000 (3,995)	35,000 (3,000)	33,000 (3,066)	21,542 (2,001)	21,000 (1,900)

255

State with the World's Largest Submillimeter Wavelength Telescope

HAWAII

Mauna Kea—located on the island of Hawaii—is home to the world's largest submillimeter wavelength telescope, with a diameter of 49 feet (15 m). The James Clerk Maxwell Telescope (JCMT) is used to study our solar system, interstellar dust and gas, and distant galaxies. Mauna Kea also houses one of the world's largest optical/infrared (Keck I and II) and dedicated infrared (UKIRT) telescopes in the world. Mauna Kea is an ideal spot for astronomy because the atmosphere above the dormant volcano is very dry with little cloud cover, and its distance from city lights ensures a clear night sky.

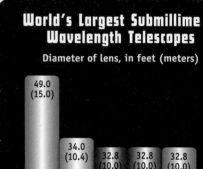

World's Largest Submillime Wavelength Telescopes

Diameter of lens, in feet (meters)

49.0 (15.0)	34.0 (10.4)	32.8 (10.0)	32.8 (10.0)	32.8 (10.0)
James Clerk Maxwell Telescope (JCMT), Hawaii	Caltech Submillimeter Observatory (CSO), Hawaii	Atacama Submillimeter Telescope (ASTE), Chile	Heinrich Hertz Telescope (HHT), Arizona	Submillimeter Telescope (SMT), Arizona

State with the Largest Human-Made Geyser

IDAHO

The human-made geyser located in Soda Springs, Idaho, shoots water 150 feet (45.7 m) into the air. The geyser was created in November 1937 when people were searching for a hot water source for a thermal-heated swimming pool. The drill dug down about 315 feet (96 m) before it hit water. The pressure—created as water mixes with carbon dioxide gas—causes the water to shoot into the air. The Soda Springs geyser is now capped and controlled by a timer programmed to erupt every hour.

United States' Largest Human-Made Geysers

Eruption, in feet (meters)

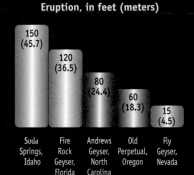

Suda Springs, Idaho	Fire Rock Geyser, Florida	Andrews Geyser, North Carolina	Old Perpetual, Oregon	Fly Geyser, Nevada
150 (45.7)	120 (36.5)	80 (24.4)	60 (18.3)	15 (4.5)

State with the Largest Cookie Factory

ILLINOIS

The Nabisco factory covers 46 acres (18.6 ha) on South Kedzie Avenue in Chicago, Illinois. The 1.75 million-square-foot (162,000 sq m) cookie factory is also one of the largest bakeries in the world. The Nabisco plant employs about 2,000 workers, and they produce about 320 million pounds (145 million kg) of Oreo cookies, Fig Newtons, and Ritz crackers each year. The factory has storage capacity for 8.5 million pounds (3.9 million kg) of flour, 2.4 million pounds (1.1 million kg) of sugar, and 1.5 million pounds (680,388 kg) of vegetable oil. There are also 20 ovens in the facility that each measure about 300 feet (91 m) in length.

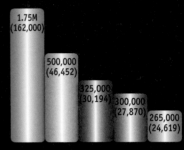

United States' Largest Cookie Factories

Area, in square feet (square meters)

1.75M (162,000)	500,000 (46,452)	325,000 (30,194)	300,000 (27,870)	265,000 (24,619)
Nabisco, Illinois	Enten-mann's, New York	Interstate Bakeries Corporation, Missouri	Interbake Foods, Virginia	Pepperidge Farm, Connecticut

State with the Largest Half Marathon

INDIANA

Cars aren't the only things racing in Indianapolis, Indiana. Each May some 35,000 runners take part in the OneAmerica 500 Festival Mini-Marathon. This makes the mini-marathon the nation's largest half marathon and the nation's eighth-longest road race. The 13.1-mile (21.1 km) race winds through downtown and includes a lap along the Indianapolis Motor Speedway oval. About 100 musical groups entertain the runners as they complete the course. A giant pasta dinner and after-race party await the runners at the end of the day. The mini-marathon is part of a weekend celebration that centers around the Indianapolis 500 auto race.

United States' Largest Half Marathons

Number of runners

Race	Number of runners
OneAmerica 500 Festival Mini-Marathon, Indiana	35,000
Rock 'n' Roll Half Marathon, Arizona	32,000
Country Music Half Marathon, Tennessee	30,000
Rock 'n' Roll Virginia Beach Half Marathon, Virginia	20,000
Rock 'n' Roll Dallas Half Marathon, Texas	13,000

State with the Highest Egg Production

IOWA

Iowa tops all other states in the country in egg production, turning out almost 14.5 billion eggs per year. That's enough to give every person in the United States about three and a half dozen eggs each! That's a good thing, because each person in America eats about 248 eggs per year. The state has 57 million laying hens, and each is capable of laying about 254 eggs a year. These hungry hens eat about 55 million bushels of corn and 27.5 million bushels of soybeans annually. In addition to selling the eggs as they are, Iowa's processing plants turn them into frozen, liquid, dried, or specialty egg products.

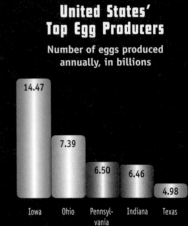

United States' Top Egg Producers

Number of eggs produced annually, in billions

Iowa	14.47
Ohio	7.39
Pennsylvania	6.50
Indiana	6.46
Texas	4.98

State with the Windiest City

KANSAS

According to average annual wind speeds collected by the National Climatic Data Center, Dodge City, Kansas, is the windiest city in the United States, with an average wind speed of 14 miles (22.5 km) per hour. Located in Ford County, the city borders the Santa Fe Trail and is rich in history. The city was established in 1872 and had a reputation as a tough cowboy town. With help from legendary sheriffs like Wyatt Earp, order was restored and the town grew steadily. Today tourists come to take in the area's history.

United States' Windiest Cities

Average wind speed, in miles (kilometers) per hour

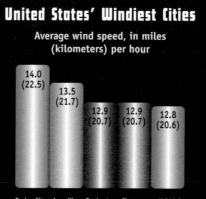

Dodge City, Kansas	Amarillo, Texas	Rochester, Minnesota	Cheyenne, Wyoming	Kahului, Hawaii
14.0 (22.5)	13.5 (21.7)	12.9 (20.7)	12.9 (20.7)	12.8 (20.6)

State with the Most Popular Horse Race

KENTUCKY

Each year, the Kentucky Derby draws more than 153,000 people who gather to watch "the most exciting two minutes in sports." The race is run at Churchill Downs in Louisville, on a dirt track that measures 1.25 miles (2 km) long. The thoroughbred horses must be three years old to race, and the winner nabs a $2 million purse. The winning horse is covered in a blanket of 554 red roses, which gave the race the nickname "The Run for the Roses." The fastest horse to complete the race was Secretariat in 1973, with a time of 1:59:40.

United States' Most Popular Horse Races

Attendance in 2009

Kentucky Derby, Kentucky	Preakness, Maryland	Breeders' Cup, California	Belmont Stakes, New York	Breeders' Cup Steeple-chase, New Jersey
153,563	77,850	58,845	52,861	50,000

Secretariat

GATOR XING
NEXT 1/2 MILE

State with the Largest Alligator Population

LOUISIANA

There are approximately 2 million alligators living in Louisiana. About 1.5 million alligators live in the wild, and another half million are raised on farms. In 1986, Louisiana began an alligator ranching business, which encourages farmers to raise thousands of the reptiles each year. The farmers must return some alligators to the wild, but they are allowed to sell the rest for profit. The released alligators have an excellent chance of thriving in the wild because they have been well fed and are a good size. Although alligators can be found in the state's bayous, swamps, and ponds, most live in Louisiana's 3 million acres (1.2 million ha) of coastal marshland.

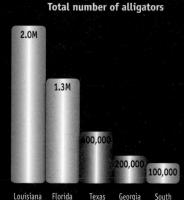

States with the Largest Alligator Populations

Total number of alligators

2.0M	1.3M	400,000	200,000	100,000
Louisiana	Florida	Texas	Georgia	South Carolina

State with the Oldest State Fair

MAINE

The first Skowhegan State Fair took place in 1819—a year before Maine officially became a state! The fair took place in January, and hundreds of people came despite the harsh weather. Originally sponsored by the Somerset Central Agricultural Society, the fair name became official in 1842. State fairs were very important in the 1800s. With no agricultural colleges in existence, fairs became the best way for farmers to learn about new agricultural methods and equipment. Today the Skowhegan State Fair features more than 7,000 exhibitors who compete for prize money totaling more than $200,000. The fair also includes a demolition derby, a children's barnyard, concerts, livestock exhibits, and arts and crafts.

United States' Oldest State Fairs

Number of years since fair first held*

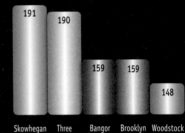

Skowhegan State Fair, Maine (1819)	Three County Fair, Massachusetts (1820)	Bangor State Fair, Maine (1851)	Brooklyn Fair, Connecticut (1851)	Woodstock Fair, Vermont (1862)
191	190	159	159	148

*As of 2010

College Park Aviation Museum

State with the Oldest Airport

MARYLAND

The Wright brothers founded College Park Airport in 1909 to teach Army officers how to fly, and it has been in operation ever since. The airport is now owned by the Maryland-National Capital Park and Planning Commission and is on the Register of Historic Places. Many aviation "firsts" occurred at this airport, such as the first woman passenger in the United States (1909), the first test of a bomb-dropping device (1911), and the first US airmail service (1918). The College Park Aviation Museum is located on its grounds, and it exhibits aviation memorabilia.

United States' Oldest Airports

Number of years open*

College Park Airport, Maryland (1909)	Robertson Airport, Connecticut (1911)	Hartness State Airport, Vermont (1920)	Middlesboro-Bell County Airport, Kentucky (1921)	Page Field, Florida (1924)
101	99	90	89	86

*As of 2010

265

State with the Oldest Baseball Stadium

MASSACHUSETTS

Fenway Park opened its doors to Massachusetts baseball fans on April 20, 1912. The Boston Red Sox—the park's home team—won the World Series that year. The park celebrated in 2004 when the Sox won the World Series again. The park is also the home of the Green Monster—a giant 37-foot (11.3 m) wall with an additional 23-foot (7 m) screen that has plagued home-run hitters since the park first opened. The park's unique dimensions were not intended to prevent home runs, however; they were meant to keep nonpaying fans outside. A seat out in the right-field bleachers is painted red to mark where the longest measurable home run hit inside the park landed. It measured 502 feet (153 m) and was hit by Ted Williams in 1946. Some of the other baseball legends who played at Fenway include Cy Young, Babe Ruth, Jimmie Fox, and Carlton Fisk.

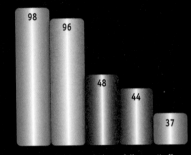

United States' Oldest Baseball Stadiums

Number of years open*

Stadium	Years
Fenway Park, Boston (1912)	98
Wrigley Field, Chicago (1914)	96
Dodger Stadium, Los Angeles (1962)	48
Coliseum, Oakland (1966)	44
Kauffman Stadium, Kansas City (1973)	37

*As of 2010

BOSTON RED SOX

State with the World's Largest Indoor Waterfall

MICHIGAN

The 114-foot (34.7 m) waterfall located in the lobby of the International Center in Detroit, Michigan, is the tallest indoor waterfall in the world. The backdrop of this impressive waterfall is a 9,000-square-foot (840 sq m) slab of marble that was imported from the Greek island of Tinos and installed by eight marble craftsmen. About 6,000 gallons (27,276 L) of water spill down the waterfall each minute. That's the equivalent of 80,000 cans of soda! Visitors can see this $1.5 million creation as they stroll through the International Center, which also houses many retail shops. Located in the historic Trappers Alley in the Greektown section of the city, the eight-story building was formerly used as a seed warehouse.

World's Largest Indoor Waterfalls

Height, in feet (meters)

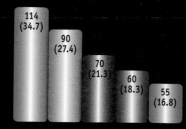

	Height
International Center, Michigan, USA	114 (34.7)
Trump Tower, New York, USA	90 (27.4)
Orchid Hotel, India	70 (21.3)
Casino Windsor, Michigan, USA	60 (18.3)
Mohegan Sun, Connecticut, USA	55 (16.8)

State with the Largest Indoor Theme Park
MINNESOTA

Nickelodeon Universe is located inside the Mall of America in Bloomington, Minnesota, and covers 7 acres (2.8 ha). The park offers 30 rides, including the Xcel Energy Log Chute, SpongeBob SquarePants Rock Bottom Plunge, Splat-O-Sphere, Skyscraper Ferris wheel, Timber Twister roller coaster, Mighty Axe, and Avatar Airbender. Some of the other attractions at the park are a rock-climbing wall, petting zoo, and game arcade. Kids can also meet Dora, Diego, Blue, and SpongeBob.

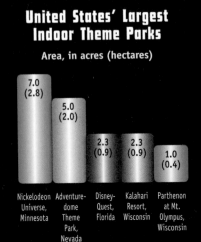

United States' Largest Indoor Theme Parks
Area, in acres (hectares)

Nickelodeon Universe, Minnesota	Adventure-dome Theme Park, Nevada	Disney-Quest, Florida	Kalahari Resort, Wisconsin	Parthenon at Mt. Olympus, Wisconsin
7.0 (2.8)	5.0 (2.0)	2.3 (0.9)	2.3 (0.9)	1.0 (0.4)

State with the Most Catfish

MISSISSIPPI

There are more than 388 million catfish in Mississippi—more than 60 percent of the world's farm-raised supply. That's almost enough to give every person in the state 132 fish each. There are about 80,200 water acres (32,000 ha) used to farm catfish in Mississippi. The state's residents are quite proud of their successful fish industry and celebrate at the World Catfish Festival in Belzoni.

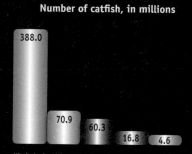

States with the Most Catfish

Number of catfish, in millions

Mississippi	Alabama	Arkansas	Texas	Louisiana
388.0	70.9	60.3	16.8	4.6

State with the Largest Outdoor Theater

MISSOURI

The Municipal Theatre in St. Louis, Missouri—affectionately known as the Muny—is the nation's largest outdoor theater, with 80,000 square feet (7,432 sq m) and 11,500 seats—about the same size as a regulation soccer field. Amazingly, construction for the giant theater was completed in just 42 days at a cost of $10,000. The theater opened in 1917 with a production of Verdi's *Aïda*, and the best seats cost only $1. The Muny offers classic Broadway shows each summer, with past productions including *The King and I*, *The Wizard of Oz*, and *Oliver!* The last nine rows of the theater are always held as free seats for the public, just as they have been since the Muny opened.

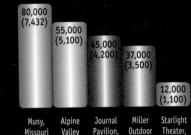

United States' Largest Outdoor Theaters

Area, in square feet (square meters)

Muny, Missouri	Alpine Valley Music Theater, Wisconsin	Journal Pavilion, New Mexico	Miller Outdoor Theater, Texas	Starlight Theater, Missouri
80,000 (7,432)	55,000 (5,100)	45,000 (4,200)	37,000 (3,500)	12,000 (1,100)

State with the Largest Bighorn Sheep Population

MONTANA

With a population of about 6,000 bighorn sheep, Montana has more of these wild endangered mammals than any other state. The population has quadrupled in the last 60 years. Many of Montana's bighorn sheep live in an area known as the Rocky Mountain Front—a 100-mile (160.9 km) area that stretches from Glacier National Park to the town of Lincoln. A ram's horns can weigh up to 30 pounds (13.6 kg)—more than all of the bones in its body. Rams use these giant horns when they butt heads with a rival sheep, and can hit each other at up to 20 miles (32.2 km) per hour.

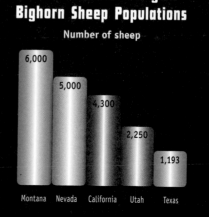

States with the Largest Bighorn Sheep Populations

Number of sheep

State	Number of sheep
Montana	6,000
Nevada	5,000
California	4,300
Utah	2,250
Texas	1,193

State with the Largest Hailstone

NEBRASKA

During a severe thunderstorm on June 22, 2003, the small town of Aurora, Nebraska, was pounded with a hailstone that measured at least 7 inches (17.8 cm) in diameter and had a circumference of 18.8 inches (47.7 cm). That's about the same size as a soccer ball. Scientists think that the hailstone was probably even bigger, but had melted some before it was preserved in a freezer. Hailstones of this size can fall at a speed of 100 miles (161 km) an hour. Sometimes hailstones can contain other objects, such as rocks, insects, and leaves.

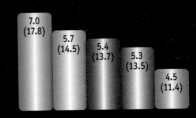

United States' Largest Hailstones

Diameter, in inches (centimeters)

7.0 (17.8)	5.7 (14.5)	5.4 (13.7)	5.3 (13.5)	4.5 (11.4)
Aurora, Nebraska (6/22/03)	Coffeyville, Kansas (9/3/70)	Potter, Nebraska (7/6/28)	Dante, South Dakota (8/21/07)	Algon-quin, Illinois (6/20/08)

State with the Largest Glass Sculpture

NEVADA

Fiori di Como—the breathtaking chandelier at the Bellagio Hotel in Las Vegas, Nevada—measures 65.7 feet by 29.5 feet (20 m by 9 m). Created by Dale Chihuly, the handblown glass chandelier consists of more than 2,000 discs of colored glass. Each disc is about 18 inches (45.7 cm) wide and hangs about 20 feet (6.1 m) overhead. Together, these colorful discs look like a giant field of flowers. The chandelier required about 10,000 pounds (4,536 kg) of steel and 40,000 pounds (18,144 kg) of handblown glass. The sculpture's name translates to "Flowers of Como." The Bellagio was modeled after the hotel on Lake Como in Italy.

United States' Largest Glass Sculptures

Length, in feet (meters)

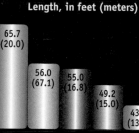

Fiori di Como, Nevada	Mille Fiori, California	Chihuly Tower, Oklahoma	Borealis, Michigan	Fireworks of Glass, Indiana
65.7 (20.0)	56.0 (67.1)	55.0 (16.8)	49.2 (15.0)	43.0 (13.1)

State with the Oldest Post Office
NEW HAMPSHIRE

Predating the Pony Express, the Hinsdale post office in New Hampshire opened its doors in 1816, and has been in operation ever since. The mail was delivered by horse and wagon, there were no paved roads, and it only cost a few pennies to send a letter. In the mid-1800s, nearby Brattleboro, Vermont, was connected to the railroad, and mail was moved by train. In 1905, the first rural route was in place and mail was delivered to some homes by horse and buggy. Today the historic building is equipped with modern technology.

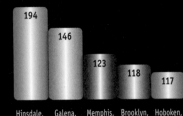

United States'
Oldest Post Offices

Number of years open*

194	146	123	118	117
Hinsdale, New Hampshire (1816)	Galena, Illinois (1859)	Memphis, Tennessee (1887)	Brooklyn, New York (1892)	Hoboken, New Jersey (1893)

*As of 2010

POST OFFICE·HINSDALE N·H·
13 MAIN STREET
03451

State with the World's Longest Boardwalk

NEW JERSEY

The famous boardwalk in Atlantic City, New Jersey, stretches for 4 miles (6.4 km) along the beach. Combined with the adjoining boardwalk in Ventnor, the length increases to just under 6 miles (9.7 km). The 60-foot-wide (18 m) boardwalk opened on June 26, 1870. It was the first boardwalk built in the United States, and was designed to keep sand out of the tourists' shoes. Today the boardwalk is filled with amusement parks, shops, restaurants, and hotels. The boardwalk recently received a $100 million face-lift, which included new roofs, signs, and storefronts for surrounding buildings. About 37 million people take a stroll along the walk each year.

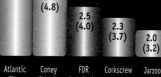

World's Longest Boardwalks

Length, in miles (kilometers)

Atlantic City, New Jersey, USA	Coney Island, New York, USA	FDR Boardwalk, New York, USA	Corkscrew Swamp Sanctuary, Florida, USA	Jarzoo Boardwalk, Sweden
4.0 (6.4)	3.0 (4.8)	2.5 (4.0)	2.3 (3.7)	2.0 (3.2)

State with the Largest Balloon Festival

NEW MEXICO

During the 2009 Kodak Albuquerque International Balloon Fiesta in New Mexico, approximately 550 hot-air and gas-filled balloons sailed across the sky. Held each October, the fiesta draws more than 760,000 spectators. This event attracts balloons from around the world, and is often seen in more than 50 countries. The festival takes place in the 200-acre (81 ha) Balloon Fiesta State Park. The Balloon Fiesta has also hosted some prestigious balloon races, including the Gordon Bennett Cup (1993), the World Gas Balloon Championship (1994), and the America's Challenge Gas Balloon Race (2006).

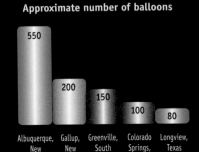

United States' Largest Balloon Festivals

Approximate number of balloons

Albuquerque, New Mexico	Gallup, New Mexico	Greenville, South Carolina	Colorado Springs, Colorado	Longview, Texas
550	200	150	100	80

State with the Longest Underwater Tunnel

NEW YORK

The Brooklyn-Battery Tunnel in New York measures 1.73 miles (2.78 km) long, making it the longest underwater tunnel in North America and the longest continuous underwater vehicular tunnel in the world. The tunnel passes under the East River and connects Battery Park in Manhattan with the Red Hook section of Brooklyn. It took 13,900 tons (12,609 t) of steel, about 205,000 cubic yards (156,700 cu m) of concrete, approximately 1,871 miles (3,011 km) of electrical wire, some 883,391 bolts, and 799,000 wall and ceiling tiles to build the tunnel. Completed in 1950, the $90-million tunnel carries about 60,000 vehicles a day.

United States' Longest Underwater Tunnels

Length, in miles (kilometers)

Tunnel	Length
Brooklyn-Battery Tunnel, New York	1.73 (2.78)
Holland Tunnel, New York	1.62 (2.62)
Ted Williams Tunnel, Massachusetts	1.60 (2.57)
Lincoln Tunnel, New York	1.56 (2.51)
Thimble Shoal Tunnel, Virginia	1.09 (1.75)

State that Grows the Most Sweet Potatoes

NORTH CAROLINA

North Carolina leads the country in sweet potato production, growing about 940 million pounds (426 kg) each year. This accounts for about 40 percent of the nation's sweet potato production. Farmers plant about 47,000 acres (19,020 ha) of sweet potato plants annually. In fact, the sweet potato is the official state vegetable of North Carolina. Oddly enough, these sweet veggies aren't really potatoes at all. Sweet potatoes are root plants—not tubers—and are actually part of the morning glory family.

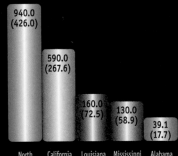

States that Grow the Most Sweet Potatoes

Millions of pounds (kilograms) grown annually

North Carolina	940.0 (426.0)
California	590.0 (267.6)
Louisiana	160.0 (72.5)
Mississippi	130.0 (58.9)
Alabama	39.1 (17.7)

State with the Tallest Metal Sculpture
NORTH DAKOTA

In August 2001, Gary Greff created a 110-foot-tall (33.5 m) metal sculpture along the stretch of road between Gladstone and Regent, North Dakota. That's the height of an 11-story building! The 154-foot-wide (46.9 m) sculpture is called *Geese in Flight*, and shows Canada geese traveling across the prairie. Greff has created several other towering sculptures nearby, and the road has become known as the Enchanted Highway. He created these sculptures to attract tourists to the area and to support his hometown. He relies only on donations to finance his work.

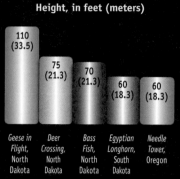

United States' Tallest Metal Sculptures
Height, in feet (meters)

Geese in Flight, North Dakota	Deer Crossing, North Dakota	Bass Fish, North Dakota	Egyptian Longhorn, South Dakota	Needle Tower, Oregon
110 (33.5)	75 (21.3)	70 (21.3)	60 (18.3)	60 (18.3)

State with the World's Largest Twins Gathering

OHIO

Each August, the town of Twinsburg, Ohio, hosts more than 3,600 twins at its annual Twins Day Festival. Both identical and fraternal twins from around the world participate, and many dress alike. The twins take part in games and contests, such as the oldest identical twins and the twins with the widest combined smile. There is also a "Double Take" parade, which is nationally televised. There are special twin programs for all age groups, since twins from ages 90 years to just 11 days old have attended. The event began in 1976 in honor of Aaron and Moses Wilcox, twin brothers who inspired the city to adopt its name in 1817.

World's Largest Twins Gatherings

Number of attendees

Twins Day Festival, Ohio, USA	Twins Weekend, Canada	"Deux et plus" Gathering, France	Mon... Can... Tw... Fest...	...wins Plus ...estival, ...ustralia
3,600	2,500	2,000	2,000	1,500

State with the World's Longest Multiple-Arch Dam

OKLAHOMA

With a length of 6,565 feet (2,001 m), the Pensacola Dam in Oklahoma is the world's longest multiple-arch dam. Built in 1940, the dam is located on the Grand River and contains the Grand Lake O' the Cherokees—one of the largest reservoirs in the country with 46,500 surface acres (18,818 ha) of water. The dam stands 145 feet (44 m) high. It was made out of 535,000 cubic yards of concrete, some 655,000 barrels of cement, another 10 million pounds (4.5 million kg) of structural steel, and 75,000 pounds (340,194 kg) of copper. The dam cost $27 million to complete.

World's Longest Multiple-Arch Dams

Length, in feet (meters)

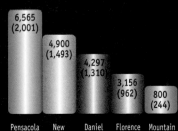

Pensacola Dam, Oklahoma, USA	New Waddell Dam, Arizona, USA	Daniel Johnson Dam, Canada	Florence Lake Dam, California, USA	Mountain Dell Dam, Utah, USA
6,565 (2,001)	4,900 (1,493)	4,297 (1,310)	3,156 (962)	800 (244)

State with the Deepest Lake

OREGON

At a depth of 1,932 feet (589 m), Crater Lake in southern Oregon partially fills the remains of an old volcanic basin. The crater was formed almost 7,700 years ago when Mount Mazama erupted and then collapsed. The lake averages about 5 miles (8 km) in diameter. Crater Lake National Park—the nation's fifth-oldest park—surrounds the majestic lake and measures 249 square miles (645 sq km). The area's large snowfalls average 530 inches (1,346 cm) a year, and supply Crater Lake with its water. In addition to being the United States' deepest lake, it's also the eighth-deepest lake in the world.

United States' Deepest Lakes

Greatest depth, in feet (meters)

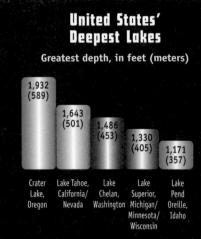

Crater Lake, Oregon	Lake Tahoe, California/ Nevada	Lake Chelan, Washington	Lake Superior, Michigan/ Minnesota/ Wisconsin	Lake Pend Oreille, Idaho
1,932 (589)	1,643 (501)	1,486 (453)	1,330 (405)	1,171 (357)

State with the Oldest Drive-in Theater

PENNSYLVANIA

Shankweiler's Drive-in Theater opened in 1934. It was the country's second drive-in theater, and is the oldest one still operating today. Located in Orefield, Pennsylvania, the single-screen theater can accommodate 320 cars. Approximately 90 percent of the theater's guests are children. Although they originally used sound boxes located beside the cars, today patrons can tune into a special radio station to hear the movies' music and dialogue. Shankweiler's is open from April to September.

United States' Oldest Drive-in Theaters

Number of years open*

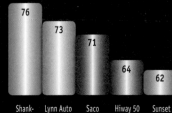

	Years open
Shankweiler's Drive-in Theater, Pennsylvania (1934)	76
Lynn Auto Theatre, Ohio (1937)	73
Saco Drive-in, Maine (1939)	71
Hiway 50 Drive-in Theater, Tennessee (1946)	64
Sunset Drive-in Theater, Pennsylvania (1948)	62

*As of 2010

283

State with the Oldest Temple
RHODE ISLAND

The Touro Synagogue was dedicated during Hanukkah in December 1763 and is the oldest temple in the United States. Located in Newport, Rhode Island, the temple was designed by famous architect Peter Harrison and took four years to complete. In addition to serving as a symbol of religious freedom, the temple played another part in the country's history. When the British captured Newport in 1776, the temple briefly became a British hospital. Then, in 1781, George Washington met General Lafayette there to plan the final battles of the Revolution.

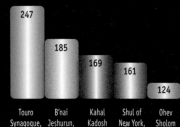

United States' Oldest Temples

Number of years since dedication*

Touro Synagogue, Rhode Island (1763)	B'nai Jeshurun, New York (1825)	Kahal Kadosh Beth Elohim Synagogue, South Carolina (1841)	Shul of New York, New York (1849)	Ohev Sholom Talmud Torah, District of Columbia (1886)
247	185	169	161	124

*As of 2010

State with the Oldest Museum
SOUTH CAROLINA

The Charleston Museum in Charleston, South Carolina, was founded in 1773—three years before the Declaration of Independence was signed. The museum was founded to preserve the culture and history of the southern town and the surrounding area, and opened its doors to the public in 1824. Some of the exhibits in the museum include furniture, silver, and art made in the area, as well as fossils of local birds and animals. Two historic houses, which were built between 1772 and 1803, are also run by the museum. Visitors can tour these homes to learn about the state's early architecture.

United States' Oldest Museums
Number of years open*

Charleston Museum, South Carolina (1773)	Albany Institute of History & Art, New York (1791)	Peabody Essex Museum, Massachusetts (1799)	Peale Museum, Maryland (1814)	Pilgrim Hall, Massachusetts (1824)
237	219	211	196	186

*As of 2010

State with the Largest Petrified Wood Collection

SOUTH DAKOTA

Lemmon's Petrified Wood Park in South Dakota is home to 30 acres (12.1 ha) of petrified wood. It covers an entire city block in downtown Lemmon. It was built between 1930 and 1932 when locals collected petrified wood from the area and constructed displays. One structure in the park—known as the Castle—weighs more than 300 tons (272 t) and is made partly from petrified wood and partly of petrified dinosaur and mammoth bones. Other exhibits include a wishing well, a waterfall, the Lemmon Pioneer Museum, and hundreds of pile sculptures.

United States' Largest Petrified Wood Collections

Area, in acres (hectares)

Lemmon's Petrified Wood Park, South Dakota	Long Logs Forest, Arizona	Rainbow Forest, Arizona	Crystal Forest, Arizona	Black Forest, Arizona
30 (12.1)	27 (10.9)	24 (9.7)	20 (8.1)	18 (7.3)

State with the World's Largest Freshwater Aquarium

TENNESSEE

The Tennessee Aquarium in Chattanooga is an impressive 130,000 square feet (12,077 sq m), making it the largest freshwater aquarium in the world. The $45 million building holds a total of 400,000 gallons (1,514,165 L) of water. In addition, the aquarium features a 60,000-square-foot (5,574 sq m) building dedicated to the ocean and the creatures that live there. Permanent features in the aquarium include a discovery hall and an environmental learning lab. Some of the aquarium's 12,000 animals include baby alligators, paddlefish, lake sturgeon, sea dragons, and pipefish. And to feed all of these creatures, the aquarium goes through 12,000 crickets, 33,300 worms, and 1,200 pounds (545 kg) of seafood each month!

World's Largest Freshwater Aquariums

Size, in square feet (square meters)

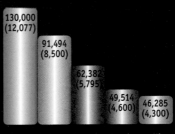

130,000 (12,077)	91,494 (8,500)	62,382 (5,795)	49,514 (4,600)	46,285 (4,300)
Tennessee Aquarium, Tennessee, USA	Freshwater Center, Denmark	Great Lakes Aquarium, Minnesota, USA	Aquarium of the Lakes, Britain	Gifu Freshwater Aquarium, Japan

State with the Biggest Ferris Wheel

TEXAS

The State Fair of Texas boasts the nation's largest Ferris wheel. Called the Texas Star, this colossal wheel measures 212 feet (64.6 m) high. That's taller than a 20-story building! The Texas Star was built in Italy and shipped to Texas for its debut at the 1986 fair. Located in the 277-acre (112 ha) Fair Park, the Texas Star is just one of the 70 rides featured at the fair. The three-week-long State Fair of Texas is the biggest state fair in the country and brings in about $350 million in revenue annually. It is held in the fall, and the giant Ferris wheel is not the only grand-scale item there. Big Tex, a 52-foot-tall (15.9 m) cowboy, is the fair's mascot and the biggest cowboy in the United States.

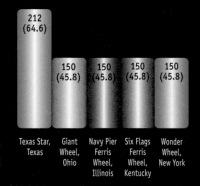

**United States'
Biggest Ferris Wheels**

Height of wheel, in feet (meters)

Texas Star, Texas	Giant Wheel, Ohio	Navy Pier Ferris Wheel, Illinois	Six Flags Ferris Wheel, Kentucky	Wonder Wheel, New York
212 (64.6)	150 (45.8)	150 (45.8)	150 (45.8)	150 (45.8)

State with the Largest Independent Film Festival
UTAH

The Sundance Film Festival in Park City, Utah, attracts more than 45,000 spectators each January. Another 1 million people watch the festivities online. Sundance has been showcasing American and international films since 1978 and has recently grown to include seminars, cultural events, and live music. The ten-day festival was originally a small event for up-and-coming filmmakers, but today it draws tons of celebrities and members of Hollywood's elite. The festival was named after Robert Redford's legendary character The Sundance Kid, since Redford's company—Wildwood—created the event.

United States' Largest Independent Film Festivals
Approximate annual attendance

Festival	Attendance
Sundance Film Festival, Utah	45,000
Independent Film Festival of Boston, Massachusetts	20,000
Rehoboth Beach Independent Film Festival, Delaware	20,000
New York International Independent Film and Video Festival, New York	15,000
Durango Independent Film Festival, Colorado	14,300

State that Produces the Most Maple Syrup

VERMONT

Maple syrup production in Vermont totaled 920,000 gallons (3,482,578 L) in 2009 and accounted for about 40 percent of the United States' total yield that year. There are approximately 2.77 million tree taps used by the state's 2,000 maple syrup producers, and the annual production generates almost $13.1 million. It takes about five tree taps to collect enough maple sap—approximately 40 gallons (151.4 L)—to produce just 1 gallon (3.79 L) of syrup. Vermont maple syrup is also made into maple sugar, maple cream, and maple candies.

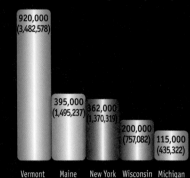

States that Produce the Most Maple Syrup

Production, in gallons (liters)

Vermont	Maine	New York	Wisconsin	Michigan
920,000 (3,482,578)	395,000 (1,495,237)	362,000 (1,370,319)	200,000 (757,082)	115,000 (435,322)

State with the Largest Office Building

VIRGINIA

The Pentagon Building in Arlington, Virginia, measures 6,636,360 square feet (616,538 sq m) and covers 583 acres (236 ha). In fact, the National Capitol can fit inside the building five times! Although the Pentagon contains 17.5 miles (28.2 km) of hallways, the design of the building allows people to reach any destination in about seven minutes. The Pentagon is almost like a small city, employing about 23,000 people. About 200,000 phone calls are made there daily, and the internal post office handles about 1.2 million pieces of mail each month.

United States' Largest Office Buildings

Size, in millions of square feet (square meters)

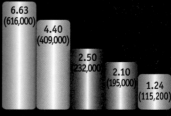

Pentagon, Virginia	Willis Tower, Illinois	Aon Center, Illinois	Empire State Building, New York	Equitable Building, New York
6.63 (616,000)	4.40 (409,000)	2.50 (232,000)	2.10 (195,000)	1.24 (115,200)

State with the Longest Train Tunnel

WASHINGTON

The Cascade Tunnel runs through the Cascade Mountains in central Washington and measures almost 7.8 miles (12.6 km) long. The tunnel connects the towns of Berne and Scenic. It was built by the Great Northern Railway in 1929 to replace the original tunnel, which was built at an elevation frequently hit with snow slides. To help cool the trains' diesel engines and remove fumes, the tunnel is equipped with huge fans that blow air while and after a train passes.

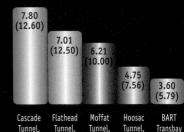

United States' Longest Train Tunnels

Length, in miles (kilometers)

Cascade Tunnel, Washington	Flathead Tunnel, Missouri	Moffat Tunnel, Colorado	Hoosac Tunnel, Massachusetts	BART Transbay Tube, California
7.80 (12.60)	7.01 (12.50)	6.21 (10.00)	4.75 (7.56)	3.60 (5.79)

CASCADE TUNNEL
7.8 MILES LONG   ELEVATION 2.247 FEET
41,152 FEET LONG   COMPLETED 1928

State with the World's Largest Teddy Bear

WEST VIRGINIA

In Charleston, West Virginia, the E.G. Bear Company created a giant patchwork teddy bear named Evan that measures 61 feet (18.6 m) tall. With an arm span of 25 feet (7.6 m), Evan could hug about 18 kids at one time. The company made the bear for an auction to benefit the Charleston Area Medical Center. The entire community helped stuff the huge, cuddly creature in November 2008. Each person who volunteered received a bucket of stuffing and the opportunity to sign a wooden heart placed inside the bear.

World's Largest Teddy Bears
Height, in feet (meters)

Evan, West Virginia	CT Dreams, Oklahoma	Warren Bear, Kansas	Jody, Kansas	York Bear, Pennsylvania
61.0 (18.6)	55.3 (16.9)	51.0 (15.5)	38.5 (11.7)	25.0 (7.6)

293

State with the Largest Water Park

WISCONSIN

Noah's Ark in Wisconsin Dells sprawls for 70 acres (28.4 ha) and includes 49 waterslides. One of the most popular—Dark Voyage—takes visitors on a twisting rapids ride in the dark. The ride can pump 8,000 gallons (30,283 L) of water a minute. Visitors can also enjoy two wave pools, two mile-long "endless" rivers, and four children's play areas. It takes 5 million gallons (19 million L) of water—the equivalent of more than 14 Olympic-size swimming pools—to fill all the pools and operate the 3 miles (4.8 km) of waterslides. Noah's Ark also boasts the country's longest water coaster (Black Anaconda), the world's longest bowl ride (Time Warp), and the world's only 4-D drive-in theater.

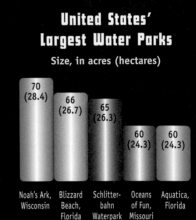

United States' Largest Water Parks

Size, in acres (hectares)

Noah's Ark, Wisconsin	Blizzard Beach, Florida	Schlitterbahn Waterpark Resort, Texas	Oceans of Fun, Missouri	Aquatica, Florida
70 (28.4)	66 (26.7)	65 (26.3)	60 (24.3)	60 (24.3)

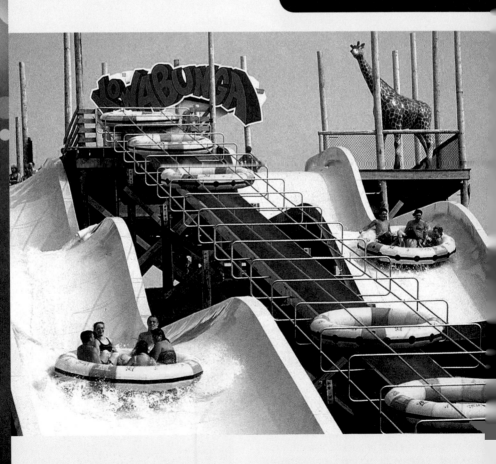

State with the World's Largest Outdoor Rodeo

WYOMING

Cheyenne Frontier Days in Cheyenne, Wyoming, brings more than 550,000 spectators to the city during the last full week of July. The festival is not only the largest rodeo in the world but also the oldest continually running. Some 1,800 cowboys and cowgirls compete for the $1 million in prize money. Besides the rodeo, visitors enjoy entertainers, a free pancake breakfast for the first 10,000 diners, and the largest parade of horse-drawn antique carriages in the world. There is also the Western Art Show and Sale featuring more than 300 paintings, bronzes, and Navajo weavings.

United States' Largest Outdoor Rodeos

Approximate annual attendance

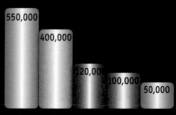

550,000	400,000	120,000	100,000	50,000
Cheyenne Frontier Days, Wyoming	The Greeley Stampede, Colorado	Reno Rodeo, Nevada	Dodge City Rodeo, Kansas	Rodeo of the Ozarks, Arkansas

INDEX

PHOTO CREDITS

OLYMPICS ■ MOVIES ■ TELEVISION

MEGA-BYTES

A Fantastic Folio of Fascinating Facts!

MUSIC ■ FOOD ■ TRAVEL

FOLLOWING THE FLAME

With a route measuring more than 279,617 miles (450,000 km), the 2010 Olympic torch relay to Vancouver was the longest in history within one country. During its 106-day journey, the torch traveled to more than 1,000 communities. Some 12,000 people served as torchbearers, carrying the propane-fueled device to every Canadian territory and province, by foot and even by Zamboni.

vancouver 2010

FABULOUS FIRSTS

There were many "firsts" for the athletes in Vancouver. Shani Davis became the first man to win back-to-back 1,000-meter Olympic speed skating gold medals. Alexandre Bilodeau became the first Canadian to win a gold medal while competing in his country. And Lindsey Vonn became the first American woman to win a gold medal in downhill skiing.

THAT TAKES MEDAL

The Royal Canadian Mint produced a total of 615 medals for the Games. There are more than 30 steps involved in the medal production process, requiring 2,817 hours (402 days!) of labor. Each medal is different, each showing a small portion of a larger original artwork. The medals were some of the heaviest ever produced, weighing from 1.1 to 1.3 pounds (0.5 to 0.6 kg).

WINTER WELCOME

Several countries made their Winter Olympics debut in Vancouver, including Cayman Islands, Colombia, Ghana, Montenegro, Pakistan, Peru, and Serbia. Two other countries—Slovakia and Belarus—won their first Winter Olympic gold medals there. Slovakia's Anastazia Kuzmina won the gold in the biathlon and Belarus's Alexei Grishin won the gold in freestyle skiing.

Alexei Grishin

WHAT'S IN A NAME?

Corporate sponsorship is not allowed in the Olympic Games, so Vancouver's General Motors Place had to be renamed Canada Hockey Place for a few weeks. In addition to the name change, the stadium was renovated to remove all advertising and make room for the media. This was also the first time Olympic hockey was played on a rink designed for NHL games, rather than with international specifications.

HEAD AND SHOULDERS ABOVE THE REST

The costumes created for the monsters in *Where the Wild Things Are* had such heavy heads, the actors could hardly stand up while wearing them. Director Spike Jonze had to send the heads back to Henson Studios to have the gigantic mechanical eyeballs removed. This meant that all the monsters' facial expressions had to be generated by computers during postproduction.

BYTES AND PIECES

In *Transformers: Revenge of the Fallen*, Devastator was created from 52,632 pieces—more than ten times the number of individual pieces in an average car. Animators needed 32 gigabytes of computer space to hold this complex creation. If all of Devastator's parts were laid end to end, they would stretch for more than 13.8 miles (22.2 km).

TRANSFORMERS
REVENGE OF THE FALLEN

LANGUAGE BARRIER

The Na'vi language—spoken by some of the characters in the blockbuster movie *Avatar*—was completely made up by linguist Paul Frommer. Director James Cameron needed a new language that did not resemble any actual language, but it had to be easy for the actors to pronounce. Frommer created about 1,000 Na'vi words.

MOVIE MUTTS

While filming *Hotel For Dogs*, trainers used more than 70 canines, which were mostly rescued from shelters. Most of the dogs were trained in less than 2 months, but the main dogs trained for more than 16 weeks. When filming ended, several members of the crew adopted some of the pooches.

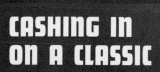

NO STRAY GETS TURNED AWAY
HOTEL FOR DOGS

CASHING IN ON A CLASSIC

The highest-grossing movie ever—when adjusted for inflation—is *Gone With the Wind*, with a $1.5 billion worldwide gross. The movie, which was released in 1939, opened in just 156 theaters. Current movies usually premiere on about 3,000 screens, yet have still failed to overtake the classic.

HOW TO SPELL THE SPELL

On *Wizards of Waverly Place*, some spells are more than they seem. For instance, the Murrieta Animata spell—which brings inanimate objects to life—was named after Peter Murrieta, the show's executive producer. Locations on the show are also named for people. Greenwald's Hardware, for example, is named after *Wizards* creator Todd J. Greenwald.

SUPERSIZED RATINGS

Super Bowl XLIV nabbed the highest viewership rating of any television show in history when 106.5 million viewers tuned in to watch the New Orleans Saints beat the Indianapolis Colts with a score of 31 to 17. About 82 percent of all televisions sets were tuned in to the game in New Orleans, and about 80 percent were watching in Indianapolis.

EXTREME EPISODES

During each episode, *Extreme Makeover: Home Edition* demolishes and creates a brand-new home for a deserving family. For every 45 minutes of TV time, there are 400 to 600 hours of footage that don't make it into the show. To build each house, it takes about 106 hours of construction, including 16 hours of framing and 4 hours of drywall. Since it began, the show has created more than 170 houses.

ROCKING THE EMMY COUNT

In 2009, *30 Rock* received a record-breaking 22 Emmy nominations—more than all of the other comedy series nominated that year combined. They went on to win five awards, including Outstanding Comedy Series and Outstanding Lead Actor in a Comedy Series. *30 Rock* stars Tina Fey and Alec Baldwin.

CHANNELING THE CHEF

The *Iron Chef America* chef with the most successful record is Michael Symon, who has won 83.3 percent of his battles. Runner-up is Mario Batali, who has won 79.2 percent. There have been more than 140 *Iron Chef America* battles since the show debuted in 2005. The chefs are told what the secret ingredient will be about 15 minutes before taping begins, so it is not a complete surprise. Whichever chef creates the better meal based on the secret ingredient wins the battle.

FIT FOR A KING

The late Michael Jackson set a posthumous record at the American Music Awards in 2009 when he won four statues, for Favorite Male Pop/Rock Artist, Favorite Male Soul/R&B Artist, Favorite Pop/Rock Album, and Favorite Soul/R&B Album. These brought his lifetime AMA wins to 23—more than any other artist in history.

SINGULAR SENSATION

With her single "My Life Would Suck Without You," Kelly Clarkson set a record for the song with the biggest jump to number 1 on the Billboard Hot 100. The song went from number 97 to number 1 after it was downloaded 280,000 times during its first week of release, in January 2009.

CASHING IN

Johnny Cash's 1958 hit "Guess Things Happen That Way" became the 10 billionth song downloaded on iTunes in February 2010. Steve Jobs and Rosanne Cash, Johnny Cash's daughter, called the man who downloaded the song to congratulate him. The 71-year-old grandfather from Georgia also won $10,000 in free iTunes music.

DOWNLOADS ARE UP

During the week of February 9, 2009, Flo Rida's "Right Round" single set a one-week sales record with 636,000 downloads. The old record was also Flo Rida's, from the previous year, when his single "Low" sold 467,000 downloads in a week. To date, Flo Rida is one of only two artists to sell more than 500,000 singles in a week (Ke$ha is the other, with "TiK ToK").

TOP TEN TUNES

Carrie Underwood made country music history in May 2009, when her single "I Told You So" topped the country charts. It was her tenth straight number-one hit off her first two albums—a feat that had never been accomplished before. The single is from her album *Carnival Ride*.

MYSTERY IS A MIX

The mystery flavor in the Dum Dums lollipop mixture is no longer a secret. Actually, the flavor is constantly changing, since it is created when one flavor is finishing production and another is just beginning. Both flavors mix together in the machine, creating the mystery pop. You never know what you might get.

STATISTICAL SWEETS

The types of homes people live in can give clues about what they might hand out for Halloween. For instance, Hershey's found that residents of houses with black shutters are 77 percent more likely to hand out Kit Kats, while people who live in two-story houses are 26 percent more likely to hand out Reese's peanut butter cups. Trick-or-treaters looking for Hershey's chocolate bars should knock on brown doors, since residents there are 32 percent more likely to give them out.

MONEY FOR MELONS

The most expensive watermelon in the world is the Densuke melon from Japan. The pricey fruit has sold for up to $6,100 at auction because it is so rare. They are occasionally available in markets for around $200. The black watermelons are crisper than the average watermelon and are grown only on the island of Hokkaido. Only about 65 melons are produced each harvest, and they are usually given as gifts.

CREAMY COLD COMBOS

Ice-cream eaters will never get bored at Cold Stone Creamery. There are more than 11.5 million possible ice-cream combinations to create there. The store offers 9 basic flavors, another 5 seasonal flavors, and about 30 local flavors of ice cream. There are about 70 mix-ins and toppings, including candy, cake, sauces, and fruit.

VAMPIRES NEED NOT ATTEND

Diners looking for some pungent treats should check out the Gilroy Garlic Festival in California each July. During the three-day event, attendees consume about 2.5 tons (2.3 t) of garlic. Some of the more unusual offerings include garlic ice cream, garlic soda, and garlic-chili syrup. The festival has used more than 75 tons (68 t) of garlic since it began in 1979.

WET IN WISCONSIN

Travelers looking to get wet should head to Wilderness Territory in Wisconsin. This is the largest water park resort in the country, featuring 500,000 square feet (46,451 sq m) of water play. The resort has 4 indoor parks, 4 outdoor parks, 100 waterslides, another 10 pools, and 2 lazy rivers. It also has one of the nation's largest indoor wave pools, at 15,450 square feet (1,435 sq m), which can hold 700 swimmers.

TOP OF THE WORLD

Each year, some 19 million visitors come to Genting Highlands Resort in Malaysia, a 10,000-acre (4,047 ha) entertainment complex that features 6 hotels with 10,000 rooms, some 90 restaurants, and 2 theme parks. And since Genting City is about 6,000 feet above sea level, guests can take a helicopter to the top or ride Asia's fastest cable car, which climbs 3,000 feet (914 m) in 30 minutes.